# BELL RINGING

# BELL RINGING

Chimes – Carillons – Handbells:
The World of the Bell and the Ringer

## John Camp

DAVID & CHARLES : NEWTON ABBOT

0 7153 6088 4

© John Camp 1974

Set in 12/13pt Centaur
and printed in Great Britain
by Latimer Trend & Company Ltd Plymouth
for David & Charles (Holdings) Limited
South Devon House  Newton Abbot  Devon

# CONTENTS

# LIST OF ILLUSTRATIONS

7

IN TEXT

# WHAT THIS BOOK IS ABOUT

This book is for those who, at present, know little or nothing about bells and bellringing but would like to know more. It is for those who love the sound of bells and may be interested in the history, customs and traditions of bellringing—an essentially English exercise, of which even most Englishmen know little.

For the majority of people bellringing appears to be an unbelievably complex subject undertaken by an eccentric few who, once a week, climb the steps to the belfry and obligingly provide a pleasing and nostalgic background to the reading of the Sunday newspapers. Who these people are remains a mystery, and what they do to produce this cascade of sound remains even more mysterious.

In the British Isles there are nearly 6,000 churches with five or more bells where Sunday service ringing is regularly performed, and the majority of these are in England. Bellringing, of the kind described here, is almost confined to Britain; the rest of the world contains less than fifty towers, most of them in Australia and America, in which the bells can be rung the English way. In Europe there are no bells rung in this manner, a remarkable enough fact when one considers the enormous

9

number of churches with bells on the continent. This phenomenon, brought about by the particular way church bells are
hung in Britain, is explained more fully in the pages that
follow.

Also explained are the basic principles of ringing, the
elementary 'handling' of the bell and the difference between
call-changes, rounds and method-ringing. But mostly this
book is concerned not with the mechanics of ringing but with
the social and historical background to the art. It describes the
evolution of church bellringing in Britain from the first
recorded bells made by St Dunstan in the tenth century,
through the vicissitudes of the Reformation, to the present
day; the coming of change-ringing and the formation of the
ringing societies; the secular use of bells after Fabian Stedman
of Cambridge had popularised change-ringing in the seventeenth century and the animosity this created between clergy
and ringers; also the Victorian Gothic revival and its effect
both on belfries and ringers. There is a chapter on the bell-
foundry and another on ringing in countries where bells have
been imported from England and hung specially. There is a
section on chimes and carillons, and a chapter on the curious
history of handbell-ringing in Britain, tracing its origins in
the seventeenth century to the great days of the handbell
rallies at Belle Vue, Manchester, in Victorian times and the
subsequent decline of the hobby and its later revival in America
and now again in England.

Finally, the book describes the customs and traditions of
ringing, the annual 'ringers' outing', the reasons for attempting
peals, odd inscriptions on bells and on belfry boards, and
the organisation of ringing today.

Despite its essential Englishness church bellringing remains
one of the most misunderstood of pursuits. This book is a
small attempt to rectify this state of affairs and to bridge the
gulf between ringer and non-ringer.

JOHN CAMP

# CHAPTER I

# BELLS IN HISTORY

The Chinese, who seem to have been doing most things longer than any other nation, are known to have used bells as far back as 4000 BC. Others before them were familiar with gongs and rudimentary bells, for the use of a curved piece of wood or metal to produce a resonant note goes back into the mists of time.

The oldest surviving bell was found at Babylon, and is reputed to be 5,000 years old. It is small, as all bells were for many centuries, and may well have been used for decorative purposes. But some of the earliest references to bells indicate that their practical value was quickly appreciated and that they were put to work in a variety of ways. According to the Jewish historian Flavius Josephus the great King Solomon made use of them in a manner still popular today—to frighten birds away from the roof-gardens of his palace. Plutarch in his *Life of Brutus* recounts that during the siege of Lycia in 42 BC bells on nets were stretched across the river to give warning of attempts to escape by water. Oddly enough, considering the future importance of bells in religion, there are few references to them in the Bible.

In European writings there is no mention of bells at all until some centuries after the establishment of Christianity.

One of the earliest references is by Gregory of Tours in 585, who talks of small bells being struck or shaken, adding that a cord was sometimes attached to the clapper. This description marks the fundamental difference between the evolution of bells in the Orient and in the Western world. In the East the bell became a hollow, round, straight-sided instrument with a sonorous tone but no distinctive note. In the West development was different, the bell evolving in the shape of an inverted cup. The clapper came to be used to a far greater extent in the West than in the Orient, where both bells and the more popular gongs were struck on the outside. Primitive bells in the West were first made of two small sheets of iron, curved and riveted at the edges and closed at the top, with a clapper inside and a handle. This is roughly the shape of Swiss cowbells today and has been the basic shape through the centuries. Bells like these were used by the first Christian missionaries to Britain, and mystic qualities were often later attributed to them. Nowhere did this mysticism find a firmer hold than in Ireland, and such bells were carefully preserved by families and handed down from generation to generation as precious heirlooms. At least fifty ancient bells have survived in Ireland to this day. Appropriately, the oldest is the bell of St Patrick himself, buried with the saint about AD 500, but later disinterred and given a superb case of silver and gold. Today it is the most precious possession of the Royal Irish Academy in Dublin. Another bell dating from St Patrick's time is the Clog na Fola, or Bell of Blood, given by the saint to a church in Connaught and said to have the power of restoring lost or stolen property. In cases of theft the bell was handed to each suspect in turn, and on it he was required to swear his innocence. If the real thief handled the bell while so doing his face would become horribly contorted and remain so until he admitted his guilt. So powerful was the mystique surrounding this bell that as late as 1850, when it was borrowed in a last-minute effort to catch a thief, the stolen goods were returned the day before the trial. Scotland, too, made use of the mystical properties of these early missionary bells. The ancient bell of St Fillian was said to cure lunacy if placed on the victim's head, but should anyone attempt to steal the bell, it would ring non-stop until returned. Bells in Scotland were sometimes used as title-deeds, and the handing over before death of an ancient and holy bell to a relative was accepted as making him the sole beneficiary of one's goods and property.

In the early Christian church small bells were used (and still are in Catholic services) at various points of the mass such as the elevation of the host. But side by side with their religious function, bells were also in extensive use for purely secular reasons. In Ireland, for example, they were rung by hand from the top of the famous tall round towers which are such a feature of many parts of the country to give warning of marauders. In time, bigger bells were used, to extend their range over the surrounding countryside, and these were pulled by ropes from the bottom of the tower. Bells were also being increased in size in Italy. Large bells were hung in the church tower and hand-bells were used for the service itself, or in processions. The first recorded mention of two distinct sizes of bell dates from AD 400, when Paulinus, Bishop of Nola in Campania, intro-duced them as part of the Christian form of worship. He described the large tower-bell as the *campana* and the small handbell as the *nola*. It is almost certainly from this nomen-clature that 'campanology' has come down to us as an alterna-tive word for 'bellringing'.

Two hundred years later Pope Sabinianus made bellringing compulsory when he ordered that the tower-bells should be rung to indicate the beginning of divine service.

Up to this point most bells had been small and rung by hand. Before the eighth century bells generally were made of iron and were not particularly musical in tone. But from about the eighth century the art of making bells from various mix-tures of alloys began to be developed, and the proportion of roughly three parts of copper to one part of tin, giving bronze, was adopted. It then became possible to cast much bigger bells with greater carrying power, and it was also discovered that by varying the thickness of the wall of the bells and also by altering slightly the composition of the bell metal, different tones could be obtained for different bells. The size of the bell also influenced its sound; the larger the bell, the deeper the note. The installation of bigger bells in church towers on a large scale began from this time, and William the Conqueror took advantage of their increased sonority by instituting the curfew bell, rung each evening at 8 pm, and still rung in some towns to this day.

Most parish churches were limited to two or three bells, though larger churches and monastic establishments had up to eight. Unfortunately no Saxon or Norman bells survive in Britain. From about the beginning of the thirteenth century a gradual alteration in the shape of the bell took place, its sides becoming longer and more concave with a consequent improvement in the tone. One of the oldest church bells in Britain is at Caversfield, Oxfordshire, and, though not dated, is known to have been presented by Hugh Gargate who died in 1219; the earliest dated bell is at Claughton, Lancashire, and is inscribed 1296. It is possible that the reason no earlier bells survived is that they were melted down and recast as the new shape gained popularity, though many vanished later at the Reformation.

As bells increased in size and weight the work of ringing them became more arduous. Various methods of doing this were evolved, without having to move the full weight of the bell to any extent. These methods, which are still used, are as follows:

*Clocking* Letting the bell hang 'dead' but swinging the clapper by means of a rope attached until it hit the side.

*Chiming* Sounding a bell: (1) by striking it on the outside by means of a hammer controlled by a rope, and (2) by swinging the bell backwards and forwards very gently to cause the clapper to hit the side when the bell was stopped.

*Ringing* Swinging the bell by a rope attached to the top, or headstock, right round and almost upside-down, then back to complete the other half of the swing. This is the standard method of ringing bells today, but with some additional refinements. One problem was how to stop the bell swinging right over if the pull was too great, and yet maintain maximum leverage. These difficulties were eventually solved by mounting the bell on a half-wheel with a rope running round it and down to the floor, and by providing a stay on the wheel's rim which, when the bell was just over its upside-down position, hit a slider in the form of a strip of timber. The slider, pivoted at one end, allowed the rest of the strip to move through a short arc, and so enabled the bell, being just over the balance, to stay upright in that position.

The final improvement was the introduction of the whole wheel soon after the Reformation. As rings were reinstalled, from the time of Elizabeth I onwards, the full wheel became normal in all towers and full control of the wheel in its movement became practicable. Thus not only was it possible to swing the bell up and allow it to 'stand' in this position for as long as was needed, but even more important was the discovery that by pulling harder on the rope as it came down the swing could be speeded, and conversely, as the bell swung up in the other direction, the rope could be retarded, making the swing slightly slower. If two ringers on two bells each carried out these manoeuvres simultaneously it was found that the bells would change places in their sequence of ringing. It was this discovery, when applied to a number of bells, that made 'change-ringing' possible; and this is the foundation on which the whole art of bellringing is based.

Though the adoption of the whole wheel was to have a fundamental effect on ringing in England, on the Continent of Europe the practice was scarcely taken up. Only in Belgium and Holland was there any real progress in this direction, but both the Belgians and the Dutch soon displayed a preference for carillons and the music they provided. The carillon is a means of ringing bells automatically, usually by a hammer striking from outside, and played from a keyboard. In this way recognisable tunes can be played, as the interval of time can be varied to the equivalent of crotchets, minims and quavers, something impossible with change-ringing where the interval is merely a fraction of a second. Another consideration is that in England the majority of churches have only six bells, making the playing of an octave impossible, and even where there are eight bells in the tower their tuning does not represent a normal octave without the addition of a sharp or a flat (see Chapter 8 on bell-founding and tuning).

Because England was the only country to adopt the full wheel, it is today the only country in the world where change-ringing and method-ringing, the most common way of ringing bells, can be practised and heard. Except for some churches in Australia, Africa, Canada and the USA, where special rings of bells have been imported from England, bellringing as we know it is essentially an English phenomenon, and is never heard elsewhere. Indeed, for nearly three centuries it was the prerogative of the Established Church, for dissenting churches and chapels normally had only one bell, and Roman Catholic churches were forbidden to ring any bells at all.

*Page 17* One of England's oldest bells at Caversfield, Oxfordshire, given to the parish church by Hugh Gargate, who died in 1219

*Page 18* (*above*) Ancient bells at Aylsham, Norfolk, rehung with new wheels and headstocks by the Whitechapel Bell Foundry; (*below*) ringers and friends from the belfry at St Giles, Reading, set out for their annual outing on August Bank Holiday, 1913

# CHAPTER 2

# THE EVOLUTION OF CHANGE-RINGING

## *The Theory*

The discovery that the order in which the bells rang could be changed without disturbing the even flow of ringing was to be a milestone in the history of campanology. From about 1630 certain ringers in London and Norwich had been experimenting with sets of these changes—called 'methods'—some of which are still in use today. But it was Fabian Stedman, a Cambridge printer, who was to investigate the full possibilities of change-ringing and to make such a vast contribution to the art. In 1668, after several years of experiment, he published in London his *Tintinnalogia—or the Art of Ringing*, in which he collected all the available information on the subject, including some new methods of his own, with the object that 'the Rules thereof may not be lost and obscured, as the Chronicles before William the Conqueror, being given only by tradition from Father to Son'. Nine years later he published *Campanologia*, his most famous volume, in which precise rules were formulated and in which there appeared details of many more of his own compositions, 'with a full Discovery of the Mysterie and Grounds of each peal'. The book was dedicated to 'The Ancient Society of College Youths' (see page 32), which association Stedman

B                                    19

had joined in 1684, and for over a century it remained the 'bible' of the bellringing fraternity.

Stedman investigated fully the total possible number of changes on any given number of bells. It is, of course, purely a matter of arithmetical permutations, obtained by multiplying the number of the bells. The maximum number of changes possible, before it is necessary to repeat one, are as follows:

| | | |
|---|---|---|
| On four bells | — | 24 changes $(4 \times 3 \times 2)$ |
| On five bells | — | 120 changes $(5 \times 4 \times 3 \times 2)$ |
| On six bells | — | 720 changes |
| On seven bells | — | 5,040 changes |
| On eight bells | — | 40,320 changes |
| On ten bells | — | 3,628,800 changes |

On twelve bells the possible number of changes reaches the astronomical figure of some 480 million, and if rung by a band non-stop would take about 36 years to perform! Allowing for meal-breaks, rest-days and holidays, it seems unlikely that any band could achieve this feat within the span of a normal lifetime.

Stedman classified peals in two ways. The first was according to the number of bells actually being used, and to these he gave the following names (see list of technical terms, page 147, for further details):

| | | |
|---|---|---|
| On four bells | — | Singles |
| On five bells | — | Doubles |
| On six bells | — | Minor |
| On seven bells | — | Triples |
| On eight bells | — | Major |
| On nine bells | — | Caters (or Quaters) |
| On ten bells | — | Royal |
| On eleven bells | — | Cinques |
| On twelve bells | — | Maximus |

Secondly he gave a separate name to each peal according to the way in which the bells changed. For it must be remembered that not only can the bells change their order of ringing 720 ways in, for example, a minor method (six bells), but the actual sequence of changes can also be varied. It is this sequence, or 'method', that determines the name of the peal. Many of Stedman's methods are picturesque in name, like 'Merry Andrew', 'A Cure for Melancholly' and 'Crambo'. Modern methods tend to be named after the church or area in which they were first rung, such as 'Cambridge', 'Bristol' or 'Kent', while the best methods that have come down from Stedman's day are still named after the composer. Thus a peal of 'Cambridge Maximus' is a peal in that particular method rung on twelve bells, while Stedman Triples is a favourite method on seven bells.

One of the rules of ringing is that a peal should consist of a minimum of 5,040 changes. This is, in fact, the maximum number of changes that can be rung on seven bells without repeating a change and is called the 'extent' of that particular number. But on less than seven bells the extent is less than 5,040; on six bells, for instance, the sequence would have to be repeated seven times to reach this figure. To avoid repetition Stedman evolved further rules ensuring that the changes would be rung in a different order each time. The order in which these changes are rung to reach the figure of 5,040 is called the method, and there are many methods used for ringing a peal on six or seven bells, or, in fact, on any given number of bells.

Though one method may be used throughout for ringing a peal of 5,040 changes, it is also possible to change from one method to another within the peal. This is called 'splicing'. The ringers at St Alkmund's, Duffield, Derbyshire, rang a peal of Spliced Surprise Major in 1972 using four different methods (Rutland, Cambridge, Yorkshire and Lincolnshire), and because of the ingenious way they were interwoven this involved ninety actual changes of method during the peal. But this is ringing of a very high and sophisticated order, and is mentioned merely to indicate the mathematical intricacies which develop from the fact that bells can be made to alter the sequence in which they ring.

So far we have dealt with the theory of bellringing. The practice is a very different proposition, and for the benefit of those who have never been in a ringing-chamber or handled a rope we shall go back to first principles and demonstrate what actually happens during ringing in the tower.

## Change-Ringing in Practice

One of the assumptions made by many writers attempting to describe the process of ringing is that the reader knows something about it already. With most learners this is not so, and as a result confusion is often caused in the early stages which retards a full appreciation of the art. Learners have been known to think that the phrase 'the bells change places' means that the bells physically change places in the belfry above, running on some kind of circular rail. Others have thought that only one person rang the bells, running from rope to rope and pulling each in turn. To those with any knowledge of ringing these ideas may appear ludicrous and, no doubt, will appear equally ludicrous to the learner after the first lesson or so. But failure on the part of those teaching to ensure that such fanciful ideas do not exist has discouraged many would-be ringers who were too shy or nervous to ask.

Over 300 years ago Fabian Stedman recommended that the learner should 'prick out' the course of a bell in a method before ringing, to understand what actually happened. This advice is as valuable today as it was then, and is undertaken as follows. From a ringing primer, copy out a simple method such as a plain course on five bells, see (a) page 23.

Now take one of the bells (say No 5), follow it through and join it up from beginning to end. You will then get a pattern as in (b). From this you will see that as soon as ringing starts, the bell begins ringing one place earlier each time ('hunting

| (a)   | (b)   |
|-------|-------|
| 1 2 3 4 5 | 1 2 3 4 5 |
| 2 1 4 3 5 | 2 1 4 3 5 |
| 2 4 1 5 3 | 2 4 1 5 3 |
| 4 2 5 1 3 | 4 2 5 1 3 |
| 4 5 2 3 1 | 4 5 2 3 1 |
| 5 4 3 2 1 | 5 4 3 2 1 |
| 5 3 4 1 2 | 5 3 4 1 2 |
| 3 5 1 4 2 | 3 5 1 4 2 |
| 3 1 5 2 4 | 3 1 5 2 4 |
| 1 2 3 5 4 | 1 2 3 5 4 |
| 1 2 3 4 5 | 1 2 3 4 5 |

down') to ring in 'first's place', and then starts 'hunting up' to the back to ring in its own place once more. Furthermore it rings twice in first's place. All the bells carry out the same manoeuvre in turn.

From this 'pricking out' the learner can discover exactly the work his bell has to do before he attempts to ring. In addition he is less likely to think that the expression 'the bell next to you' refers to the ringer standing next to him in the tower. It does not. It means the bell which is ringing next to his in that particular change, and it may or may not be that of his neighbour. There is no excuse for a ringer beginning to ring while he is still confused by this. If this happens it is failure on the part of his teacher. Yet the fact remains that the degree of confusion existing amongst learners is far higher than many teachers admit. Unfortunately, as in so many disciplines, expertise in a subject bears little relationship to the ability to teach it. Far too many able ringers have far too little patience, and the 'born' ringer who had little difficulty in mastering the first principles of the art cannot understand that others (who may be far more intelligent in other ways) cannot pick it up as quickly as he did. This happens in many towers, and despite the constant lamentations that are heard about the shortage of ringers and the difficulty of finding recruits it is unfortunate that many young people have been discouraged by the superiority sometimes displayed by proficient and experienced ringers. In this respect ringing is rather like driving a car—it rarely brings out the best in people!

The way in which ringing is carried out in the tower is illustrated diagrammatically below. The rope is attached to the wheel at a point on the grooved circumference and runs down through a hole in the floor to the ringing chamber below. Here the rope terminates in about three feet of fluffy, coloured material, called the 'sally', used for getting a better grip and also as a visual aid for determining the position of the bell in its swing.

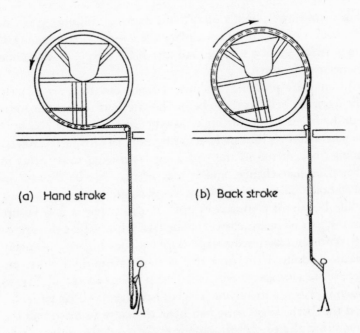

(a) Hand stroke    (b) Back stroke

Showing position of bell rope at hand stroke and back stroke

FIGURE 1

When the bell is 'set', that is upside down and resting in a position just off balance, a pull on the rope will cause it to come off balance and swing downwards, and if the pull is maintained gently it will swing up the other way. If, at this point, the rope is checked slightly just before the bell reaches its second upside-down point, it will swing back and up to its original position. If checked again it will swing down once more. Continuous ringing is achieved by repeating this pulling and checking of the rope in turn so that the bell swings backwards and forwards in a steady rhythm. Each ringer doing this in turn results in the bells ringing in sequence from the lightest (the treble) to the heaviest (the tenor) and is called 'ringing in rounds'. If you look at diagrams (a) and (b) again you will see that in (a) the rope runs straight off the wheel and down through the hole, giving a long length of rope in the chamber below; but when the wheel swings round to the other position (b) the rope is wound round about half the circumference of the wheel before going through the hole, so considerably shortening the length of rope in the ringing chamber. The first pull of the rope (a), when the sally is on the floor or may even have to be doubled up on the rope, is called the handstroke, and the second pull, with the sally above face-level, the backstroke (b).

The art of handling a bell, therefore, is to cause it to swing backwards and forwards without letting it come to rest between strokes, and this can be achieved only with practice on a given bell. If the rope is retarded too much as the bell swings up, it will start coming down again too soon, and if insufficiently retarded, the stay on the wheel is likely to hit the slider hard and may even snap it, causing the bell to turn over again in another revolution and wind up the rope in the process. This can be a very alarming experience for a learner, whose instinct is to try and keep hold of the rope and pull the bell back. This is virtually impossible to do, and more than one learner who has clung to his rope has been lifted into the air and dropped back on the ringing-chamber floor. Fortunately there is little risk of this happening as learners are never allowed to handle a bell without supervision, and are never put on the heaviest bells to begin with. Once the proficient handling of the bell has been mastered, with due regard to the position of the feet and an erect posture, then ringing in rounds can begin. The ringer then learns how to retard his bell slightly to allow another bell to ring before it, and how to speed it to ring in front of another bell. It is important that the bells ring in an even and steady sequence, with the same interval of time between each sound; this is known as good striking, and is pleasant to listen to.

At the beginning of his training the new ringer will not be expected to ring methods, but will gain experience in 'call-changes', a system whereby the captain allows the ringing to continue in rounds for a little while and then 'calls' a change, instructing two bells to change places. This change may then continue for some time before another is called. This is valuable experience for the new ringer, and he has little to remember until he hears the number of his particular bell called and the number of the bell he must change with.

In method-ringing, of course, the bells change places every time they ring, and the ringer must remember the sequence of these changes to perform efficiently. Yet it is not as hard as it might appear, and it is not necessary to memorise a series of 5,040 changes individually to ring a peal. We must go back again to the method of 'pricking-out' the path of the bell on paper, for the particular method to be rung and memorise the pattern it makes. By linking up these sequences of patterns, and with the help of certain rules and mnemonics, a peal of 5,040 changes (which usually takes just over three hours) can be accomplished without too much strain. The conductor of the peal, who knows the method intimately, is also able to signal instructions and call when the learner has gone wrong, to put him back on the right path and bring the peal to a successful conclusion. Sometimes the mistake is too serious to be rectified and as the work of each bell is interlocked with the others the whole peal collapses and comes to a jangling end.

Few things are more frustrating to a ringer than to find that the peal is going wrong after nearly three hours of ringing, with only fifteen or twenty minutes to go. But it happens to everyone. Saddest of all was the peal attempt that failed after two and a half hours when a ringer's trousers began to slide gently to the floor.

The ability to ring methods without fault is assessed differently in various parts of the country. In the London area, and over most of the south of England, proficiency in method-ringing is rated very highly, and the *Ringing World* (the weekly journal of ringers) records each week the peals and quarter peals attained by bands of ringers in churches up and down the land. But in the West Country it is different. There, proficiency in striking is thought of very highly, and for this reason many experienced ringers in Devon and Cornwall rarely ring methods but only call-changes, though their striking is a delight to listen to. As far as the general public is concerned there is little doubt that good striking is more satisfactory to the ear, and the change has time to register on the memory before the next one is called. In method-ringing this is not always so, and the listener outside the church is conscious only of a continual alteration in the sequence without having any appreciation of the art and dexterity going on in the tower. The value of both systems of ringing will always be a matter of contention; probably the ideal is proficient change-ringing coupled with perfect striking, an accomplishment not often heard in the average parish church. If the sound of the bells is intended to bring the faithful to worship it should be as attractive a sound as possible, and good ringing of rounds is infinitely preferable to a cacophonous attempt at a method; regrettably, this view is not shared by the majority of tower captains outside the West Country.

The work of the tenor bell must be mentioned. The majority of churches in England have six bells, yet the favourite method of ringing is 'doubles', rung on five bells. In such a method

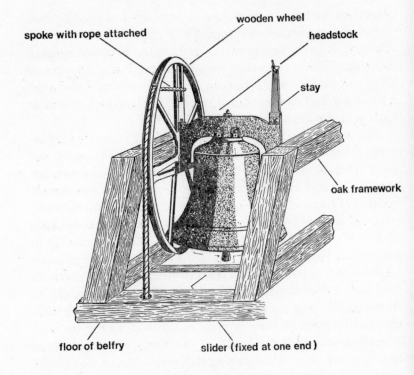

spoke with rope attached

wooden wheel

headstock

stay

oak framework

floor of belfry

slider (fixed at one end)

### *Bell hung for change ringing*

FIGURE 2

the first five bells (from treble downwards) actually perform the method, the tenor bell ringing 'behind' in its proper place at each change and never varying. This ringing of the tenor at the end of each change imparts a steady and regular rhythm, breaking up the sound into bars, as in music and it also serves as a metronome to the ringers themselves, enabling better striking to be performed. A good 'tenor-man' is a valuable adjunct to any band, though too often written off as having more brawn than brain. The tenor bell, as the heaviest in the ring, certainly demands more stamina than the other bells, particularly where the tenor does not ring behind, but takes part in the method itself. To speed and retard the tenor and allow it to do the normal work allotted to it in a peal demands the full resources not only of a strong ringer but also of an experienced one, for the slightest mistake can result in chaos. If a tenor ringer can negotiate a peal of 5,040 changes without error, and still impart a steady rhythm with good striking, he is very good indeed.

Before any ringing can start, however, the bells must be raised from their normal position mouth-downwards to the upside-down position described earlier. The rope of each bell is pulled, gently at first, causing the bell to swing in ever-widening arc. As the bell swings higher and higher the clapper finally hits the side of the bell and it begins to sound. If all the bells are being 'rung-up' (as it is called) the sound should be in the normal order of ringing from treble to tenor, and the ideal is to make these sounds as perfectly spaced as possible. It must be remembered that because the bells are swinging through a short arc the sound comes very much faster. The technique of 'ringing up in peal' is therefore a difficult process, for while the interval between the sounds gradually gets longer and longer as the bells rise there should be the *same* interval between each bell until they are all up. Ringing down the bells after a service is the reverse procedure, but even harder, as less control is possible when the bells are falling. The tenor is usually rung up and down separately.

# The bell ringing cycle

THE BELL HERE IS DOWN

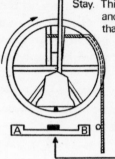

Direction of movement when the rope is next pulled

Stay. This catches against the slide and stops the bell turning more than one revolution

Slider. This is fixed at one end. The other rests on a beam and is pushed by the stay from A to B or reverse at each stroke

THE BELL IS NOW UP AT HAND STROKE

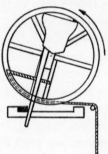

Direction of movement when the rope is next pulled.

The stay has pushed the slider to the limit of its movement and the bell cannot turn any further.

THE BELL HAS NOW SWUNG RIGHT ROUND AND IS NOW 'UP' AT BACK STROKE

Direction of movement when the rope is next pulled

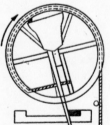

FIGURE 3

# CHAPTER 3

# THE RINGING SOCIETIES

The practice of hanging bells in churches had become established in England long before the invention of the half-wheel and Stedman's later studies in change-ringing and its complexities. From the time of the Norman Conquest, when William inaugurated the ringing of the curfew, bells played an increasing part in the life of the people. In churches up and down the country they called the faithful to prayer—not only on Sundays, but every weekday—to matins, mass and evensong. Bells were rung 'at ye cumyng of ye bischop and of ye king ye quene and ye prince', to quote instructions to deacons at Coventry in 1462. In addition (say the same instructions) the deacon shall 'grese ye bells and find grese thereto, and see to the bawdricks and clapers and the bell rope in lyke manner'. All in all, the duties of the deacon in maintaining the bells were fairly onerous, even in a parish church where there may have only been two or three bells. In an abbey or cathedral church the care of the bells inevitably became a full-time job, and equally inevitably those engaged in the work formed themselves into 'gilds', partly the better to administer the work and share the labour, and partly to protect their working conditions. During the reign of Henry III (1216–72) there began a massive rebuilding programme of many of England's larger churches, and it is from this period that the Early English style of architecture belongs, with its pointed arches and flying buttresses, replacing much of the severity of Norman architecture. In this building and rebuilding the bells played an important part, and it was during the rebuilding of Westminster Abbey at this time that we find the first record of a guild of ringers. This was 'The Brethren of the Gild of Westminster', who were officially recognised in a Patent Roll of Henry III in 1254, though they must have been ringing some years before that. Similar guilds were formed elsewhere in later years, including the guild of Holy Trinity, Coventry (1462) and the 'Gild of St Pauls' (1507).

Such guilds were formed by and for those engaged in ringing at specified churches and included only those employed by the church, for ringing was a paid job. In 1254 the Gild of Westminster ringers were receiving a payment 'out of our Exchequer' of a hundred shillings, fifty at Easter and fifty at Michaelmas.

The coming of change-ringing, made possible by the wheel and half-wheel, drew the attention of many who were not so much interested in church affairs as in the art of ringing as a hobby, or as an exercise—and, indeed, it is as 'the Exercise' that it is known to this day. Then, as now, it was the young who were attracted to this new diversion and who banded themselves into associations for the sole purpose of practising the art. One of the earliest societies was that of the 'Schollers of Chepesyde in London', founded in February 1603 according to Narcissus Luttrell writing in 1682. There must have been many such societies in the early years of the seventeenth century, but few records remain.

The oldest secular ringing society still in existence is generally agreed to be the Ancient Society of College Youths, founded in London in 1637. The college which the Youths attended was the College of the Holy Ghost and Hospital of God's House, itself founded by Master Richard Whittington in 1424, in Upper Thames Street in the City. This was the famous Dick Whittington of pantomime fame, though he was in fact Lord Mayor of London four times, not three, as legend has it.

In their early days the College Youths were the more aristocratic students of the College, presumably those who were less concerned with study than with doing the smart thing of their day. Founder members included Lord Brereton, Sir Cliff Clifton, the Marquis of Salisbury, Lord Dacre, and the sons of many city aldermen, all of whom assiduously practised rounds and call-changes 'to promote the art of ringing'. Stedman himself, who was by then a well-known ringer, joined the society in 1664 and dedicated his *Tintinnalogia* to its members in 1668.

The Society of College Youths rang regularly at St Bride's in Fleet Street, at St Lawrence in Jewry, at Westminster Abbey and many other London churches, mainly in the City. St Bride's seems to have been one of their favourite centres, and it was in this church that they rang the first peal of Grandsire Cinques in 1724, the first peal of Bob Royal in 1725 and the first peal of Maximus in 1726. They rang at Canterbury for the first time in 1732, and even crossed the Channel to ring handbells in Calais during the same trip. They rang more handbells on the way back 'when half-seas over'!

Despite this show of adventurous spirit the Society later acquired a name for slowness and conservatism, so much so that by the end of the eighteenth century a splinter group, calling itself the Junior Society of College Youths, had been formed. It did not last long and two years later all its members were back in the fold and the Society flourished once again, with several notable peals to its credit.

Today the Ancient Society of College Youths, together with the Society of Royal Cumberland Youths (see page 34), forms the élite of the bellringing world. Its members are responsible for ringing at St Paul's Cathedral and Westminster Abbey; membership is by invitation only and restricted to the most proficient and practised ringers. Its very handsome Certificate of Membership was designed by the famous eighteenth-century engraver Bartalozzi and one of its trophies is a silver cup presented in 1783 for winning a striking competition at Sonning, Berkshire. The annual dinner of the Society is still a major event in bellringing circles and takes place in London in early November. Though the colourful procession from its former headquarters in Gresham Street to Bow Church for divine service has been discontinued, the custom of toasting past masters of the Society 'of 300, 200 and 100 years ago' still survives. Not that all members are remembered entirely for their prowess on the bells! An unfortunate incident occurred in 1786 when the Society visited Norwich, then as now a famous ringing centre. The Norwich ringers rang a touch of Stedman Cinques, a method unknown to the London ringers, who, when they returned home, left Thomas Blakemore behind to learn the method so that he could later impart its mysteries to his own society. Blakemore lodged with an eminent Norwich ringer, Christopher Lindsey, who was engaged in writing a treatise on the art of ringing. Blakemore, it seems, copied out the entire manuscript, unknown to Lindsey, and on his return to London published the work as his own, entitling it *Clavis Campanologia*. The truth of this story was doubted by that erudite historian of ringing, the late Jasper Snowdon, but the fact remains that in the list of subscribers to *Clavis Campanologia* (1788) not one name of a Norwich ringer appears.

The Society of Royal Cumberland Youths was founded in 1747 with headquarters at St Leonard's, Shoreditch. Tradition has it that the Society was formed from an older association called the London Scholars, dating from about 1710. The Scholars were ringing the bells of St Leonard's one day in 1746 to welcome the Duke of Cumberland on his return to London after the Jacobite rising of 1745, and the Duke, himself a keen ringer, was charmed by the bells and complimented the ringers on their proficiency, presenting a medal to them the following year. In commemoration of this gesture the name of the society was changed to the Royal Cumberland Youths, and the Duke

*Page 35* Ringers about to 'pull off' at St Margaret's, Wellington, Herefordshire

*Page 36*
(*left*) Tom Tower at Christchurch College, Oxford, from which 'Great Tom' rings each evening to call the scholars home; (*below*) the unusual detached bell-tower at the church of St Mary, Pembridge, Herefordshire

later presented a large oil painting of himself to the Society.

Because of the site of their 'home' church in Shoreditch the Cumberlands numbered many Huguenot immigrants amongst their members. That they were a wealthy association is evidenced by the fact that in 1807 they were able to present two more bells to the church to make a ring of twelve, the Duke himself having augmented the ring from eight to ten some thirty years earlier. The parish church of St Leonard's, Shoreditch, is still the home of the Cumberlands, though members ring all over the country, as do the College Youths. In London itself, however, they are responsible for ringing at St Martin's-in-the-Fields and at St Margaret's, Westminster.

It goes without saying that the existence of two such eminent ringing societies in London created a rivalry that persists to this day, though each society invites the other to its functions and dinners. The following verses aptly underline this long-standing feud.

### A Tragic Ballad

It is of an old gent I'll have you to know
Who rang at St Paul's and at Cornhill also.
He lived all alone with young William, his son,
Who was promising well, though not yet forty-one.

One evening the father admonished young Will:
'You must come down to practice tonight at Cornhill,
For afore you reach sixty, if no ill befalls,
I believe I could get you a ring at St Paul's.'

'Oh Father, dear Father,' young William replied,
'I can't tell you lies, though you know how I've tried—
I've promised tonight (and I mean to be there)
For to ring at St Martin's in Trafflegar Square.'

'My son,' quoth the sage, 'do not enter that tower—
You never shall ring with that horrible shower!
You'll change your mind quickly, avoiding disgrace,
When I tell you it's CUMBERLANDS ring in that place!'

Said William, 'A young lady ringer I've met
And on her my affections most firmly are set.

C

Your rooted objections to me are no barrier
For I love her, dear Father, and I'm going to marry 'er!'

'Now, William,' said Father, 'just listen to me
For if you insist it's cut off you will be,
And when I expire and am laid into dust
I'll leave all my cash to the Barron Bell Trust.

'I've rung all my life, and I still must insist
That what you're describing can't ever exist.
I've heard people tell that there's women what ring—
But a *lady*—why, no, boy, there ain't no such thing.'

Next month they were married, that couple so bold,
And the poor father's grief was a sight to behold.
His brain is quite gone, the psychiatrist thinks,
For he even goes wrong in three courses of Cinques!

But Will and his bride, also sad to relate,
Just could not escape from the vengeance of Fate.
When poverty pressed, their possessions they sold,
And now live in Devon, near Itch-in-the-Fold.

And there they are forced to go up in the tower
Ringing rounds and call-changes for hour after hour.
But even that fate ain't as bad as it sounds—
For they *could* be in Cornwall—and only ring rounds!   (*Anon*)

Though Cumberlands and College Youths were the predominant ringing societies in London in their day they were not the only ones. There were also the Prince of Wales Youths (1788), the Eastern Scholars (1733), the Society of London Youths (1753) and the Westminster Youths of about 1800, to name only a few.

Outside London, two of the earliest societies were the Croydon Youths (1734) and the Wye Ringers of Kent who recorded their first peal in 1736. These, of course, were local ringers. Of the larger societies whose activities were not confined to one church or area, the two oldest still in existence are the Saffron Walden Society of Essex, formed in 1623, and the Society of Ringers of Lincoln, 1612.

Probably because of Stedman's association with the district, East Anglia has long been a noted ringing centre, and Norwich a mecca for generations of ringers. Yet it is not the cathedral that today provides the ringing, for its bells have been hung 'dead' (ie capable of being struck only, not swung) since about 1800. It is on St Peter Mancroft, that most wonderful of English churches, that the Exercise is centred. But though the already formed London societies were visiting Norwich as early as 1680 to learn more of the art, it was not until 1716 that the ringers of the city formed themselves into an association. This was a year after the first-ever true peal on church bells was rung at St Peter Mancroft on 2 May 1715, and since that time Norwich ringers have remained in the forefront of the Exercise.

In the context of ringing today, societies and associations fall into four categories. First come the diocesan guilds formed from parish church ringers in each diocese. Akin to them are the county associations of parish churches. Next come the 'secular' associations, which include the ancient societies such as Cumberlands and College Youths, whose members are not drawn from any particular area and whose ringing is not confined to any particular district. Both Oxford and Cambridge universities have a century-old association of ringers, and the modern universities have also formed ringing associations which in most cases are flourishing, though with inevitable wastage as undergraduates complete their academic careers. Lastly comes the more modern phenomenon of what might be termed 'trade associations'—in which members of one profession or calling find a common meeting-ground for the practice of ringing. The Guild of Medical Ringers, for example, has been in existence officially since 1955, though the first peal rung by an entirely medical band was at Abbots Langley, Hertfordshire, in 1947. There is a Guild of Masonic Ringers, a Police Guild, a Railwaymen's Guild and a Guild of Post Office Ringers; there is news of a teachers' ringing association being formed, as well as of one whose members are all estate agents!

There is one ringing association that stands apart from these four categories: the Ladies' Guild, formed in 1912. Women had been ringing in increasing numbers since Miss Alice White of Basingstoke became the first lady ringer in 1896. That their presence was welcomed is indicated by a ditty of the day that ran:

> Like a breath of summer laden, like a cheery ray of hope,
> Is the sight of gentle maiden deftly handling of a rope.

Ringing evidently had an equally beneficial effect on the ladies themselves, for Miss White, who was the first president of the Ladies' Guild, is still alive, and ninety-three, at the time of writing. Today women and girls take their places side by side with men in most towers, for, despite the popular view, bell-ringing does not require Herculean strength or an excess of stamina.

Those who join an association are usually keen and dedicated ringers and are looking for an opportunity to enjoy the art beyond the confines of the once-weekly practice in their own church or service-ringing on Sundays. And here we meet the conflict of opinion that has been such a feature of ringing ever since the College Youths formed themselves into a secular society 300 years ago. Should ringing be confined to service-ringing only, or may it be indulged in purely as a hobby and an exercise? To most people the answer seems comparatively simple. The main object of ringing is for the glory of God and to call the faithful to prayer; it does at the same time demonstrate to the non-church-goer that services *are* being held and that people are attending them. But there is no reason why the art should not be practised and perfected whenever possible to increase the standard and quality of ringing on Sundays. Yet, as so often happens with matters religious, misunderstandings continue and multiply whenever the subject is discussed, as reference to the pages of the *Ringing World* amply demonstrates.

The printed record of peals rung shows a curious sense of guilt in many of those who give reasons for ringing. It seems as if ringers, wishing to attempt a peal or even a quarter, must have some justification for doing so, in case ringing for ringing's sake should be thought sinful! In 1960, for example, the ringers of Rothwell, Northamptonshire, rang a peal 'to commemorate the 100th anniversary of the return of Fydor Dostoyevsky to St Petersburg after ten years' exile in Siberia'! (Several weeks later correspondence in the *Ringing World* was still continuing as to whether or not the Russian writer could be accurately termed a 'revolutionary' as he died nearly forty years before the 1917 revolution.) In 1972 the Guild of Post Office ringers decided to ring a peal at each of the five churches depicted on a recent issue of 'parish church' stamps. But perhaps the most practical reason for ringing the bells was given by an inn-keeper ringer of Hereford who lost his beer-licence in 1871. The aggrieved publican, unable to continue in business, collected his fellow-ringers and proceeded to ring non-stop during licensed hours as a sign of protest at the decision of the magistrates. Said the *Ledbury Free Press*, with righteous indignation: 'This is the grossest belfry outrage we ever heard of.' The protest was effective, for the licence was renewed at the next sessions.

CHAPTER 4

# RINGERS AND THE CLERGY

The College Youths in London and the flourishing ringing societies in Norwich, Lincoln, York and other cathedral cities all helped to increase the status of ringing during the seventeenth and eighteenth centuries and to raise its status to that of an art. True, there had been a setback during the Commonwealth, for Cromwell and his followers did not encourage ringing. At Deddington, near Banbury, the church bells were bought by the parliamentary troops and melted down for shot, as a result of which the villagers benefitted financially and were able to remain drunk for three weeks afterwards. But in most churches the bells remained *in situ*, and were just not rung.

The Restoration revived ringing throughout the country. Not only did it give an opportunity for the serious practitioners to improve their techniques, but it also provided a fine excuse for anybody and everybody in the village who thought he could ring a bell to join the band in the belfry and earn himself a few shillings. No opportunity to ring was lost, and the belfry in many cases became the social centre of the village. Beer was always on tap, cursing and swearing was rife, and there was a total disregard of the fact that ringing was predominantly a religious function and that the tower, bells and ringing-chamber were all part of the church building and under the control of the incumbent and churchwardens.

The bells were rung to announce the opening and closing of the weekly market, and on the squire's birthday; later, to herald the arrival of the stage from London, as well as for the more legitimate purposes of announcing deaths and funerals. November the Fifth was celebrated with peals in many country churches, as was the anniversary of Trafalgar. Church bells were used to signal the beginning of the racing season, the start of the local statute fair, the beginning of harvesting and the safe arrival of the last load home.

Private individuals with money to spare occasionally hired the ringers to signal an important event, and frequently donated money to the tower in thanks for peals rung. In an age when travel was perilous, roads often impassable and street lighting non-existent, more than one traveller was saved from an untimely death in swamp or bog and was able to gain the roadway again by following the sound of the church bells. At Wingrave, Buckinghamshire, in 1732 a certain Mrs Elizabeth Theed almost lost her life in a storm while trying to make her way home across the fields from the nearby village of Rowsham; the sudden ringing of Wingrave's church bells enabled her to find her direction again and reach safety. In gratitude she gave a field to the church in perpetuity, directing that each year, on the anniversary of the event, hay from the field should be strewn on the church floor for the better comfort of the faithful. The custom is maintained to this day. Again, in 1753 a Mr William Davies of Twyford, Hampshire, was saved from falling into a chalkpit while on a nocturnal jaunt by the sound of the local ringers at their weekly practice. He provided money for the ringers for an annual breakfast in thanksgiving, and his bequest is still enjoyed by the ringers of Twyford, though practical considerations have transmuted it from breakfast to an evening function.

But of all those who paid for the bells to be rung in thanks for deliverance from peril, the prize must surely go to Thomas Nashe of Bath. On his death in 1813 this cynical individual left £50 to the abbey ringers to ring a 'muffled and funereal peal' on the anniversary of his marriage, and directed that 'a grand Bob Major and merry mirthful peals to commemorate my happy release from Domestic Tyranny' should signal the anniversary of his demise!

With the bells being run for any and every occasion, villagers might well have voiced their discontent at the constant clamour as loudly as do members of the Noise Abatement Society today. But in fact it was the clergy who objected most strongly to this misuse of church property, and in particular to the goings-on in the belfry itself. Not that it had much effect! In the smaller communities, where everyone was related to everyone else, too outspoken a criticism would have led to unpopularity and a sudden decrease in the already dwindling attendance at church. The money earned by the ringers was spent locally in the village inn, for ringing was notoriously thirsty work, and this circulated in the community. There were other and more practical considerations too. In most churches the captain of the ringers had the key to the belfry, and the tower was treated more as an annexe to the church than part of it, with the incumbent only grudgingly allowed entry. Not that many of the clergy demanded access, for they became disillusioned with the situation and knew they were fighting a losing battle. They were thankful if the ringers graciously condescended to ring for service on Sundays, even if it was virtually unknown for any ringer to attend the service.

By the beginning of the nineteenth century the 'monotonous link which binds together the Belfry and the Beerhouse' was well and truly forged, and none knew how to break it. Everything had been tried, from locking the belfry door against the ringers to fining them for misusing church property, a situation that arose in Thurnby, Leicestershire, in 1820. Needless to say no fines were paid, though the rector pursued the matter to the extent of seeing the ringers languishing in jail in default. In the event the fine was eventually paid—by the rector himself!

Even in towns, where the ringers were usually better organised and mostly members of a ringing society, they could also be difficult. Here they often showed their disapproval of unpopular measures by withdrawing their services, as they did at High Wycombe and other places in 1832 on the occasion of the annual visit of the bishop to mark their displeasure at his voting against the Reform Bill in the Lords.

But help was at hand—and from an unexpected source. In 1833 the Reverend John Keble, then Professor of Poetry at Oxford, preached his famous Assize Sermon in the university town. Together with his friends Newman and Pusey he advocated a return to the ritual and pageant of the pre-Reformation church and a move away from the drabness that had characterised the Church of England since then. Improvements and redecorations were needed with structural alterations involving the chancel, nave and aisles. Not that the congregation was consulted in any of these alterations. Most parishioners deplored the wholesale destruction of so much that had become familiar to them, but there was little they could do. Protest was left to the church bellringers, for included in the alterations in many churches were changes to towers and ringing-chambers. These changes, in an area of the church not normally visible to the congregation, were carried out by the architects not only as part of the reversion to the Gothic style, but often at the request of the incumbent in an attempt to bring the ringers more under control. Ringing-chamber floors were removed and the ropes lengthened so that the bells were rung from the floor of the tower, often within the sight of the congregation. Many bells were re-cast and re-hung, often on ball-bearings, to make ringing easier and reduce the need for refreshment. In those places where in addition the ringers could not leave the tower without going through the church, the cries of protest from the older ringers were loud and long. They created difficulties whenever possible and brought to a head the long existing feud between ringers and clergy. As late as 1865 an article in *The Ecclesiologist* was headed 'Successful Tactics of a Country Curate with an Ungodly Set of Ringers', and in many churches the ringers were actually forbidden to ring for Sunday service, their behaviour being considered inappropriate to the house of God.

Part of the trouble, of course, was that for a long time the clergy had taken no interest in the bells or belfry and had refused to contribute to their maintenance. The ringers, as a result, took no interest in the church services and refused to support the incumbent. When, as a result of the activities of the ecclesiologists, the clergy attempted to reassert their presence in the belfry they frequently met with a hostile reception. A Warwickshire curate who went to visit the ringers after practice recorded: 'But the men, not understanding my motive, did not appreciate my presence and gave me several hints that they preferred my room to my company. The fact was, they had never been accustomed to have a "gentleman" amongst them, and the parson's presence was decidedly an uncomfortable check upon their usual free and easy mode of procedure.'

But gradually opposition died down as the older generation of ringers vanished and new ringers took up the Exercise. The easier handling of the bells made it possible to ring longer and more complex touches before service, and, towards the end of the century, was responsible for the appearance of women ringers. Earlier the Camden Society had sent representatives round churches to interview ringers and to persuade them to adopt higher standards of behaviour in belfries. They suggested revised rules of conduct, the appointment of a tower captain, and more liaison with the incumbent. The same Warwickshire curate whose presence in the tower had been so greatly resented was able to write later: 'Our belfry, which was once the resort of the idle and profane, has now become regarded as it should be—a holy place.'

Yet even today the war is not quite over. Few incumbents are actively hostile to the ringers but there are still far too many who take the ringing of bells on Sunday for granted and never spare a thought or prayer for the ringers themselves. On occasions such as Harvest Thanksgiving and Easter, when grateful thanks are given from the pulpit to all those who have contributed in decorating the church or assisting in other ways, it is rare for the ringers to be mentioned. At Christmas, when representatives of local organisations are chosen to read the lessons in turn, not often does one hear a lesson read by a ringer. Too often ringers are mentioned only when they fail to be present or perform inadequately. The result is to engender in some ringers the attitude of earlier times. The situation could be improved in many churches were the incumbent to show a little more interest in ringers and ringing. He cannot be expected to take up ringing himself (though there are many clerics who are accomplished ringers), but at least he could visit the ringing-chamber occasionally on practice night and bring the ringers more into the ambit of church activities by acknowledging their contribution. Very slowly this is happening, and in some churches, even, the old joke may be paraphrased and the 'captain of the ringers will be found hanging in the porch'. In the meantime the pages of *Ringing World* continue to demonstrate that the old argument of secular versus religious ringing continues. Perhaps most significant is a recent announcement from a parish priest that he intends selling the bells for salvage unless they are rung more often!

# CHAPTER 5

# PROBLEMS OF TOWERS AND BELFRIES

The Camden Society and all it stood for exerted a profound effect on church architecture throughout the latter half of the nineteenth century. As far as the church-going public was concerned it created a greater interest in the design of churches and in so doing made congregations more aware of what bell-ringing involved. In the belfry itself the effect was to make ringers more knowledgeable about the mechanics of bells and to arouse a greater awareness of the construction and maintenance of bells and towers.

During the nineteenth century the opportunity had been taken to augment many rings from four bells to five or six as churches were restored, and to provide new churches with rings adequate for good ringing. In the rapidly expanding London suburbs and in the industrial areas of Lancashire and Yorkshire new churches were being built at an astonishing rate, but unfortunately, in many cases, by men with only a sketchy knowledge of the problems created by the ringing of bells and the consequent movement of several tons of metal in a tower. Not surprisingly the medieval builders (who had overcome so many problems in their time) had been well aware of the difficulties involved, and had Victorian architects bothered to examine the bells and towers of the churches they were restoring, instead of concentrating almost exclusively on the more visible parts of the fabric, they would have learned a great deal and avoided many later errors. There was little in print to point the way apart from an occasional article in *The Ecclesiologist* (the journal of the Camden Society, later called the Ecclesiological Society) and it was not until 1910 that Sir Arthur Heywood wrote the first book on the subject. Even more surprising is the fact that today, over sixty years later, no other book has been published for the guidance of architects on those matters except for the recently published *Towers and Belfries* of the Central Council of Church Bell Ringers. So Victorian architects were almost working in the dark when dealing with bells and this is the reason why today, in the 7,000 churches in Britain known to have rings of bells, some 1,500 are classed as 'unringable'. The fault, in most cases, is not in the condition of the bells themselves, but that the structure of the tower makes continued ringing a danger.

The strains and stresses exerted by a number of bells ringing simultaneously is enormous. In a six-bell tower the total weight of the bells when hanging 'dead' may be between 3 and 4 tons, a weight easily supported by the tower walls as the stress is downwards. But when the bells begin to swing the strain is greatly increased. At the bottom centre of its swing, when it is travelling at maximum speed, a bell exerts a downward force equal to four times its normal weight, and a horizontal force twice that weight. If the bells were hung side by side in the tower, all swinging in the same plane, the total effect would be far greater than any masonry could stand and disaster would result—as, indeed, happened in Liverpool in 1810 when the tower disintegrated during Sunday morning ringing!

Bells are therefore hung in a frame large enough to accommodate them all, but arranged in such a way that when they are ringing the stresses are opposed and virtually cancel out. The frames in which the bells are hung were formerly made of timber—huge rock-hard beams that may still be seen in many country churches today. But as nineteenth-century renovation to belfries continued, they were replaced by iron frames which were much more rigid and less likely to transmit the stress from the swinging bells to the masonry. Though there remains a school of thought that affects to see some advantage in the greater 'elasticity' of timber bellframes, modern designers hold that absolute rigidity of the frame is essential. In many cases when they were rehung bells were fitted with ball-bearings instead of plain bearings, thus making the work of the ringer considerably easier.

The wooden wheel on which the bells are mounted must also be considered most carefully, as it helps to support a great weight and is subject to its own stresses and strains. It is therefore of the utmost importance that the bells and their gear receive adequate maintenance, and in most towers one person has responsibility for this. Included in the gear are such things as the slider and stay, which stop the bell from turning right over at the end of its swing, and also the clapper, normally of wrought iron, which strikes the bell on each side in turn during ringing at the same two points. The moment during the course of the swing at which the clapper strikes the bell is determined by the weight and length of the clapper and also by its shape. The clapper is pivoted to an iron loop in the crown of the bell and can swing only in a plane parallel to the swing of the bell. But constant contact with the side of the bell can eventually cause wear, and if the pivot of the clapper is worn there will also be a slight 'roll' every time it hits the bell which will eventually cause a small indentation. For this reason it is customary to re-hang bells every few years and replace them turned slightly so that the clapper does not hit the same part of the bell for too long.

The ropes by which bells are hung are a most important part of belfry equipment. These are normally made of Italian hemp, a material strong enough to withstand constant wear as the rope passes up and down through the garter-hole in the belfry

floor to the ringing chamber below, yet supple enough to
negotiate the acute bends imposed on it and not to fray or fly
off the wheel when in action. Perhaps its most important
characteristic is that it must not become elastic during use and
must not be affected by weather or temperature change.
Materials other than hemp have been tried, but all have their
drawbacks. Nylon lasts a long time and resists abrasion, but is
elastic, as well as being hard on the hands. Sisal frays too easily,
and jute is not strong enough.

In towers where ringing is carried out from floor level and
the bells are high in the tower the length of rope is considerable.
Such a tower is said to have 'a long draft' and can be dangerous
for the novice if no rope-guides are provided in the ceiling:
when travelling up and down during ringing the ropes can
'snake' to an alarming degree unless kept taut, and in such a
tower more than one ringer has found a loop of rope entwining
his arm or head and has extricated himself only just in time to
avoid being hauled aloft. Fortunately, experienced ringers are
well aware of these hazards, and no learner would be asked to
ring a bell under such conditions without somebody standing
by him ready to take the rope in a crisis.

A crisis of another kind, however, is sometimes caused by
the presence of new ringers in towers. The noise they make can
create a great deal of ill-feeling towards ringers particularly in
densely populated areas. Obviously, a new ringer must be
taught how to ring, and during the first few nervous lessons he
is likely to make a noise on his bell which will fray the nerves
of those who have to listen. The problem is partly overcome by
tying the clapper during the first few practices so that the bell
makes no sound when it is swinging. During this period the
learner is taught how to handle his bell, how to keep control
of the rope as it speeds up and down, how to let the bell rest
gently on the slider at the top of its swing, and to get the
general feel of his bell so that later he may be able to concentrate on the sound of it without being conscious of the move-
ments he is making. Most learners acquire this aptitude after

only a few lessons, and the day comes when the bell is untied and the clapper swings free. But—oh horror!—what has happened? The bell once again seems uncontrollable and the learner finds he is creating more cacophony than he ever thought possible! What has happened, in fact, is that the bell moves differently when the clapper is untied, with disastrous results. But if the learner perseveres for another lesson or so he will quickly accommodate this different movement, and will have taken the first step to becoming a proper ringer. Even so, of course, his striking will be at fault for many months to come, and this will transmit itself to those listening outside as a jangle and unmelodious sound, for good striking is the essence of good ringing. Only practice will improve this, during which time many local residents will no doubt join the Noise Abatement Society or even write to their MPs.

Whilst it is true to say that in most towns the church and bells have been there very much longer than the surrounding houses, most ringers do what they can to mitigate this nuisance. Practices are held usually only one night a week and ringing ceases by 9 pm at the latest. Another more permanent method of reducing the noise is to fit special reversed louvres to the belfry windows so that the sound goes upwards instead of downwards. The use of soundproof cladding throughout the belfry is a better way of dealing with the problem, for the reversing of the louvres to let the sound travel upwards also allows rain into the belfry.

Many of the complaints concerning the excessive noise of church bells are based not on the volume of sound but on the harshness and general discord produced. This is much more difficult to circumvent, as it may be caused not only by keen young ringers learning to handle a bell but be owing also to the time-honoured practice of hanging bells as near as possible to the belfry windows, resulting in an irregular and discordant note from these outside bells compared with the sound from others placed farther away. The latter problem can be solved only by a major rehanging of the bells, something that takes

*Page 53* The detached timber belfry-cage at St Mary the Virgin, East Bergholt, Suffolk; (*below*) the famous handbell ringers of Launton in the US Air Force chapel at Upper Heyford, Oxfordshire, recording a programme for American TV

THE CLAPPERS OF THE OLD RING.
OUR DUTY DONE IN BELFRY HIGH,
NOW VOICELESS TONGUES AT REST WE LIE.
PRESERVED BY EDWARD ARCHER 1837

*Page 54 (above)* The clappers of the old bells preserved at the Priory Church of Great Malvern, Worcestershire; *(below)* the parchment scroll of 1716 listing the Articles of the Norwich Ringers' 'Purse Society' hanging in St Peter Mancroft, Norwich

place in most parish churches only at an interval of many decades. In the meantime ringers can quieten opposition by keeping strictly to advertised times of ringing on practice nights.

Without wishing to labour the point it must also be said that good striking in rounds or call-changes is infinitely preferable to attempts at peals by inexperienced ringers, particularly on Sundays. Though it may well be true that the church has been there longer than the houses that surround it, this is no defence in law if it is established that a nuisance has been held to be created. Many ringers are unaware of this ruling.

One way of reducing the discord occasioned by learners is to take advantage of one of the courses on bellringing held in different parts of the country. The Lincoln Diocesan Guild, for example, runs a weekend residential course under the auspices of the Kesteven Education Committee for both beginners and advanced ringers, and deals with a wide range of subjects from the elementary handling of the bell in the tower to the technicalities of conducting and 'proving' methods.

Since 1963 the Hereford Guild has also run a three-day annual course which includes lectures on bell-hanging and belfry maintenance and attracts students from as far afield as London and Scotland. But it was not until 1971 that a course devoted to tower and bell maintenance only was inaugurated, this time by the Guild of Devonshire Ringers who took students round various towers in the Exeter area and gave practical demonstrations on the working and maintenance of such items of belfry gear as clock-hammers, and on correct lubrication and the splicing of bellropes. It is hoped that maintenance courses will be started in other areas, for it is only through familiarity with the mechanics of bellringing that good ringing can be achieved and bad striking and discord reduced to a minimum.

D

CHAPTER 6

# SOME UNUSUAL TOWERS

The internal and external design of churches has always been a matter on which the public are peculiarly sensitive. Experiment in a truly modern idiom has only come to be accepted in the last few decades. Before that anything which did not conform to the old ideas of how a church should appear was severely criticised, some of the most outspoken critics being those who rarely went to church services. 'Design' meant a constant harking-back to the past, and those architects brave enough to attempt using modern materials in a modern way, while yet preserving a religious atmosphere, often ended by pleasing nobody. Yet parish churches throughout the British Isles display a wide variation in architectural style, and architects of a former age were often surprisingly unconventional in the way they set about solving problems.

The sudden awareness of bellringing and the subsequent increase of bells in many parish churches during the sixteenth and seventeenth centuries imposed problems, not the least being the additional weight church towers were called upon to carry. Strengthening and even complete rebuilding of towers was carried out, and in some instances the tower was moved to another part of the church. This happened at High Wycombe, where the original central tower was demolished and rebuilt at the west end during the early years of the sixteenth century. It is a tall and dominating structure, well able to withstand the movement of its twelve bells. High Wycombe is interesting, too, in that it has a thirteenth bell (a 'sharp' second) included in order to provide a complete octave, with accidents, for use with the carillon that regularly plays hymn tunes for the delight of the townspeople.

Most churches have their towers at the west end, but occasionally a central tower creates problems for ringers. At Corley, Warwickshire, the bells are hung in a curious little timber turret in the roof above the nave and the ropes drop down on to the pews below. Where it is performed in a church with a central tower, ringing is often done from the chancel or chancel steps, an arrangement that only the most extrovert ringers enjoy. This happens at Roade, Northamptonshire, at Lympne in Kent, at Ickleton in Cambridgeshire and at Winsham in Somerset, to name only a few. At Ottery St Mary the bells are rung from the south transept, and in the historic church at Chicheley, Buckinghamshire, the ringers perform from what must be one of the few remaining rood-lofts.

Even where there are reasonable ringing conditions many architects seem to have overlooked the purely physical problems of reaching a high ringing-chamber from ground level. Most of us are familiar with the worn spiral staircase that wends its way aloft from the tiny door at the foot of the tower. But at Cottingham, near Hull, where the stairway is narrower, darker and more worn than most, it terminates in the belfry itself, amid the bells; ringers then have to go down again through a trapdoor level with the bellframe to reach the dungeon-like ringing-chamber below. Merton College chapel, Oxford, has no ringing-chamber proper but a 3ft wide stone gallery round the walls of the tower. The floor is 60ft below with nothing in between! There are eight bells, including a 28cwt tenor, and from the bells the ropes come down to the ringers at an incongruous angle, making control difficult. A similar situation formerly existed at Southwell Minster,

Nottinghamshire (an anti-clockwise ring), but a belfry floor was installed there in 1963.

At Long Melford, Suffolk, the beautiful parish church is at long last suffering from the unconventional installation of its eight bells, which are hung neither in the usual clockwise manner, nor anti-clockwise, but diagonally. Cracks have recently appeared in the masonry of the tower and ringing is restricted while a sum is raised additional to the £50,000 target already required for structural repairs to the nave.

Long Melford, a famous church in a wealthy area, will no doubt achieve its target. Less fortunate are hundreds of smaller churches in remote areas where the chances of raising money for repairs are slight. It remains a curious anomaly that while the financial resources of the Church of England may be used for building new churches, no funds are allowable for the repair of existing buildings. This is the reason for the constant fund-raising schemes for church repairs which are encountered in almost every parish in the country. It accounts, too, for the silencing of many splendid rings—from that at Norwich cathedral to A. E. Housman's bells at Bredon, which no longer 'sound so clear'.

At Darfield, in the West Riding of Yorkshire, and at Hatfield in the same county, mining has caused dangerous subsidence which has effectively put an end to ringing. On the other hand ringing continues in many belfries where the oscillation of the tower causes concern to those ringing there for the first time. Famous is Worcester's All Saints, whose incumbent wrote in 1911: 'When the full peal of ten bells is rung the tower sways perceptibly from the top to the foot, causing even the ink in my vestry inkstand to shimmer.' Since then the bells have been rehung twice, in 1914 and again in 1951, but the wobble remains. The basic cause is the height of the bells in the tower, which has a direct effect on the oscillation, and the faulty arrangement of the bells vis-à-vis their swing. Chesterfield's famous twisted spire, caused by warping of timbers under the lead tiles and producing a twist 8ft out of true, was scheduled for demolition as dangerous in Victorian times, and again in 1961. But it is still there—all 228ft of it—and likely to remain.

There is an almost infinite variety in the shape of towers, belfries and ringing chambers, and each church has a character of its own. Some have achieved fame through outside circumstances; others, like the church of All Saints at Maldon, Essex, with its unique triangular tower and its ring of eight, were unusual from the first. Probably the most bizarre ringing-chamber is at Pershore Abbey, Worcestershire. It is situated in the lantern tower of the abbey (begun in 1330) and consists of two beams sprung from the massive walls and meeting in the centre, 72ft above the floor of the church. On this structure has been placed a wrought-iron cage 12ft square, each of whose corners lies opposite the centre of a wall, so producing a diamond effect when seen from below. Perched here the ringers ring the great bells immediately above them, including a tenor of 28cwt, and arrive in the cage via a narrow stairway in the wall, up an openwork flight of iron steps 21in wide, and finally along one of the supporting beams railed up on each side. It is not unlike ringing in the Royal Zoological Society's aviary in London.

Towers *have* fallen down, both in town and country, sometimes through neglect and sometimes through rough handling by ringers. The tower of the church of Hempstead, Essex (where Dick Turpin was born), collapsed in 1882; the new tower dates from 1962.

One of the most interesting attempts to prolong the life of a tower was made in Horley, Surrey, in 1970. Here a completely new tower of iron was built *inside* the old timber one, and a new bellframe installed. There were many critics of this revolutionary technique, and, indeed, their opinions seemed justified at the dedication of the bells, which was notable for the uneven and 'bumpy' ringing. But immediate attention rectified the matter, and though it is too early to forecast how ringing will eventually develop there seems every indication that the experiment has been a success. This is important for Horley, for originally it was intended to demolish the church. With an enlightenment that is rarely encountered in parochial church councils it was agreed that if the tower and bells (a particularly fine ring of eight) could be saved, then a new church would be built adjoining it. And this was what happened. Small wonder that the ringers of Horley are fiercely sensitive to any criticism of their bells, rare as it is for bells and tower to be the means of preserving a church.

## Detached Towers

When the addition of bells to a tower seemed to endanger the structure, builders of a past age sometimes built a special ringing-tower adjacent to the church. There are about twenty such detached towers in Britain, mostly with heavy rings. One of the best known is at the church of All Saints and St Laurence near the market-place at Evesham, Worcestershire, which carries a ring of twelve bells, including a 35cwt tenor. There is another not far away at Ledbury, in Herefordshire. One of the most famous detached rings, and the subject of many postcards sent home by holidaymakers to East Anglia, is housed in a low timber cage in the churchyard at East Bergholt, Suffolk. These bells are not mounted on wheels or pulled by ropes.

At Bury St Edmunds, again in Suffolk, the heavy 30cwt tenor with its nine companions hangs in the great tower of the former Norman abbey. St David's cathedral, at the western tip of Wales, rings its bells from an ancient gatehouse in the grounds. There is a curious situation at Swaffham Prior, in Cambridgeshire, where two churches sit side by side in one churchyard. One church is derelict, but preserves its tower and bells which ring regularly for services in the other church, which has a tower but no bells. Brookland church, Kent, has an extraordinary-looking detached timber pyramid as a bell-tower.

In Scotland one of the most interesting detached towers is at Inveraray, Argyllshire. Bells in Scottish churches are hung mainly for chiming, and few can be rung in the orthodox manner. The first complete ring of bells in Scotland was not installed until 1788, by the Whitechapel Bell Foundry, for St Andrew's Church, Edinburgh. Even today Scotland has only thirteen usable rings in a total of nearly seventy towers. Most have been installed during the last hundred years, and the detached tower at Inveraray was completed in 1931 alongside the Episcopal church built in 1886. The ring of ten enormously heavy bells was cast by Taylor's of Loughborough in 1920, and with their 41cwt tenor forms the second heaviest ring of ten in the world after the ten at Wells Cathedral. Though the tower at Inveraray is still separated from the church this was not the original intention, but funds have never been sufficient to complete the work. The tower and bells fell into disuse after the war, but in 1970 a band of volunteers, including local schoolchildren, cleaned and scraped the bells and frame while experts examined the bell-gear and put it into ringable condition. An extremely active and publicity-conscious association called 'Friends of Inveraray Bells' then went into action to raise funds for maintenance and general improvement, and Inveraray is well on the way to becoming a major Scottish tourist attraction. This far-sighted association allows the public to visit the bells and belfry every day during the holiday season, and visitors are urged to join the association as well as to buy souvenirs of the bells and literature on ringing. A highly successful LP recording of the bells has been made and a second is being arranged. In 1972 close on 4,000 people visited the tower.

## Secular Ringing Towers

While detached towers are found in various parts of the country, most of them still have the original church adjacent to them. But there are cases where the church no longer exists and only the tower remains. Carfax Tower, in the centre of Oxford, is one such; and though the bells here are rung regularly the original church of St Martin of Tours has long vanished. St Leonard's Tower, the famous tower at the crossroads in the centre of Newton Abbot, Devon, is another example of a tower with no church. It was built in the thirteenth century and was once part of the parish church of Wolborough, on the south bank of the river Lemon. On the north bank was Newton Bushel, again with its own parish church. By the early 1800s the twin villages had combined and grown to form the nucleus of the thriving market town we know today. St Leonard's church was far too small to accommodate the increased congregations, and there was no room to extend it in the busy town centre. It was therefore demolished and a larger parish church built some distance away. But the tower and its bells remained, though through the years it suffered from neglect. Again, volunteers began a fund-raising scheme, and there is every hope that it will soon be possible to undertake a complete rehanging of the eight bells and that their sound will once more be heard over the Devon countryside. It seems there will be no shortage of ringers, for the local members of the Devon Constabulary, to say nothing of the Devon Guild, are ready and willing to man the ropes.

Newton Abbot tower and Carfax Tower were originally church towers but are now secular (the base of Carfax Tower is now used as an Information Centre). But several ringing towers exist which were never associated with any church, and were built purely for secular use. One of the oldest of these is the clock tower at St Albans, Hertfordshire, erected in 1403. With only two bells it cannot really be included in a list of towers where there is proper ringing, but the bells themselves are interesting, and the larger of the two is older than the tower itself, being cast in 1335. It weighs a ton and is known as Great Gabriel. Though the clock tower never had anything to do with the Abbey of St Albans and was not under its jurisdiction, it is thought that the bell may have originally been part of the abbey ring. As installed in the clock tower Great Gabriel became a curfew bell, ringing each night at 8 pm and again at 4 am to rouse the apprentices for work. This practice was discontinued in Victorian times after a petition from the townsfolk, and today it is limited to striking the hours and being 'clocked' at the death of a monarch. Morpeth, Northumberland, also has an ancient watch tower, with a ring of eight bells, all in good condition, and was never associated with a church.

Church-towers which have been deconsecrated and are now used for secular ringing include St John's Church, Micklegate, York, now the Institute of Advanced Architectural Studies, and the church of St Mary at Quay in Ipswich, Suffolk, which has recently been handed over to the Boys' Brigade.

## Privately-owned Ringing Towers

Modern towers built purely for ringing are few on Britain. The best-known is the campanile at Taylor's bell-foundry at Loughborough (one of the only two bell-foundries in Britain) whose ten bells are said to have been rung more than any other bells in England. Manchester Town Hall has a world-famous ring of twelve bells hung for ringing with another twelve in use as a carillon, the hour bell weighing over 8 tons. The total weight carried by the tower is 42 tons.

The town hall at Berwick-on-Tweed has a ring of eight bells in its tower, though unfortunately these are unringable, and in London the Imperial College in South Kensington has a massive ring of ten bells, including a 38cwt tenor, installed in its Queen's Tower.

Whilst the dedication and enthusiasm of bellringers is well known few have been so married to the Exercise as to build a ringing tower solely for their own use and at their own expense. One man who did so, however, was John Powell the squire of Quex Park near Birchington, Kent, who in 1819 erected the Waterloo Tower, complete with twelve bells, in the grounds of his home. The tower itself is a fine example of the Gothic style then much in vogue, topped with a spire of curly cast-iron.

The official description issued at the time explains that the intention was that the spire would make 'a noble sea mark, being only one mile from that briny fluid'. Both Cumberlands and College Youths were invited to the opening ceremony, to which ringers came from all over the country, and no doubt the festivities caused some perplexity to mariners who heard the continuous sound of the bells whilst sailing on 'the briny fluid' off the Kent coast. The tower is still there, and the bells are rung regularly by members of the Kent Association and by visiting bands.

For 150 years the Waterloo Tower remained the only privately owned purpose-built ringing tower in Britain, but within the last few years others have been built, though not on the lavish scale of Quex Park. In 1951 Charlie Jarvis, a farmer at Balscott near Banbury, and a lifelong ringer, decided to build a tower on his land and provide a ring of bells. They were six in number initially, a predictably light ring with a 1¾cwt tenor. For an ordinary ringer with no particular technical or scientific training the hanging and arrangement of bells is an extremely difficult undertaking, and at Balscott the problem was increased by the very lightness of the ring. The conventional timber wheels were not possible, for example, and the ingenious Mr Jarvis at first used bicycle wheels of varying sizes for the purpose. The first six bells were cast by Gillett & Johnson, a Croydon foundry that no longer undertakes this work though it still engages in hanging and maintenance, and they were an instant success. In 1961 the ring was augmented to ten, and was later increased, first to a complete ring of twelve and subsequently, with ancillary bells added, to a total of sixteen. The lightest bell weighs a mere 14lb. The bells are now hung in a solid metal frame on aluminium wheels, in exactly the same way as church bells. In 1971 Mr Jarvis retired and built himself a bungalow on a hilltop site in Balscott, adjacent to the tiny red sandstone village church. Behind the bungalow is a long, low shed of the sort used for agricultural equipment, and at its western end a 20ft tower, green-painted and clad with corrugated iron sheets, where Mr Jarvis has now installed his beloved bells. The ringing chamber, 11ft by 10ft, has a low ceiling through which emerge the ropes, each with its gaily coloured sally. A ladder leads up to the belfry, and here one is confronted with an astonishing sight. The bells hanging there are arranged scientifically to reduce stress to a minimum, each on its wheel and complete with slider and stay, exactly as in a church tower. Mounted above them are the four small bells that have recently been installed, the whole representing an incredible achievement by a man who claims he has no technical knowledge but has just 'listened to other people talking'. The sound of the bells is high and sweet, with a surprisingly mellow tone for such small dimensions.

The village church has two bells only, and the Jarvis bells are rung regularly for weddings by members of the Banbury branch of the Oxford Diocesan Guild; they are also becoming increasingly popular with touring bands. Each bell has been individually cast for Mr Jarvis, the later ones by the White-chapel Bell Foundry, and bear his name.

Only in one other place in England can anything comparable be found. At Stoulton in Worcestershire a local resident, Arthur Jopp, has made a collection of old school bells, had them tuned to a complete ring of six, and hung them in the first floor of a cottage adjoining his house. Here, again, they are hung in a proper manner on frame and wheels, as in church, and until Mr Jarvis installed his latest light bells, were claimed to be the lightest ring of six in the world. But Mr Jopp is also planning to augment his ring, and there is much friendly rivalry between the two men. In the meantime the ringing fraternity benefits from the incredible enthusiasm, industry and skill which have led to the installation of two private rings of bells, the only ones to have appeared in Britain during the last century and a half.

# CHAPTER 7

# THE EXERCISE IN ACTION

In Britain today there are estimated to be between 50,000 and 60,000 active ringers, and the number is growing. They range from dustmen to doctors, from eleven-year-olds to octogenarians and from those with deep religious convictions to those who prefer to define a church as 'a building attached to the bottom of a belfry'. Because ringers are drawn from such widely divergent types and social classes, bellringing is often described as the most democratic of all pastimes. The captain of the ringers in a country church may well be a farm labourer and the latest recruit the local solicitor or doctor. Democratic as it is, it is no more so than cricket, bowls or other activities where the outcome depends on team effort. The great difference between the team effort required in ringing and that involved in other activities, however, is that in ringing every member of the team is performing at the same time. It is also non-competitive. Ringing together as a band produces a situation where the difference between the expert and the learner becomes immediately and clangingly apparent. Unfortunately, while expert ringers are plentiful, expert teachers are not, and far too many tower captains have far too little patience with learners; moreover, while ringing is in progress instructions to the learner have often to be shouted to be heard, a practice unlikely to increase self-confidence. Expert method-ringers, or 'scientific' ringers as they are sometimes called, are often curiously insensitive people, impatient with those less proficient than themselves and intolerant of other ringers' views and opinions. They are not always mentally suited to impart the secrets of the art with success or efficiency. The learner should be aware of this paradox, and wherever possible take instructions not from the expert ringer but from those only a little more advanced than himself.

## The Central Council of Church Bell Ringers

Whether or not the ringer is religiously inclined, he will be exercising his hobby in a sacred building and inevitably will learn something of church affairs. Church bellringers are organised in diocesan guilds and new recruits are encouraged to become guild members. Ringing matters at national level are controlled by the Central Council of Church Bell Ringers who issue publications of a technical nature, ranging from their *Beginners' Handbook* to a booklet on towers and belfries intended principally for architects. They also publish the bellringers' official journal, the weekly *Ringing World*, which has a circulation of about 7,000 but a readership probably five times that figure.

*Ringing World* was founded in 1911 by John Goldsmith, who was also its first editor. It was intended to act as a focal point for ringers' views, and to give them a platform for their opinions. Most important of all, as an experienced newspaper man Goldsmith intended that his new journal should 'publish all news while it is still news and not when it has become history'. Goldsmith remained editor for over thirty years, and was succeeded during the difficult days of World War II by J. Arminger Trollope who in turn vacated the editorial chair in 1946 for Thomas White. Twenty-three years later, in 1969, Charles Denyer became editor, the fourth in a period of sixty years.

Each week *Ringing World* publishes a list of quarter-peal and peal attempts by bands up and down the country. These are not included merely as a matter of interest but as a record of achievements which may be collated and analysed as the years pass by. New compositions are recorded and vetted by the Central Council, and many peal attempts indicate the reason for ringing on that particular occasion and record it officially, with names of those taking part.

The Central Council also formulates the rules of ringing and claims for new methods are scrutinised carefully to ensure that they are really new and that no rules have been broken and they are therefore not false. A new method must be given a name, usually the area or town in which it was first rung, or more rarely, the name of the composer. From time to time there appear in the pages of *Ringing World* names that were obviously not intended to be taken seriously. In 1972 some consternation was caused by the submission of two new methods, one named 'Boghole Surprise Major' and the other 'Fanny Bedwell'. For the next few weeks the correspondence columns were spattered with expressions of 'filth', 'disgusting' and 'obscene' from the more staid ringers, and cries of 'so what?' from the younger element. One can only feel sympathy with the scrutineers of the Central Council whose job it is to verify such claims; only a close examination of a gazetteer of the British Isles will indicate whether or not a place called Boghole really exists. After all, Stevenage New Town *has* got a Bedwell Happy Wives Club!

## Peal-Boards and Instructions to Ringers

The *Ringing World* is not the only place in which peals are recorded. In the tower itself the successful attempt at a peal or quarter-peal is often indicated by a peal-board on the wall. Many of the older boards are of great historical interest. One in St Peter Mancroft, Norwich, records the first-ever peal of Grandsire Triples rung on 26 August 1718. Also in this church is a large painted parchment, dating from 1716, which lists the articles of membership of the Norwich Scholars' Purse Club, or Benefit Society, which for many years dominated ringing in the city.

In addition to peal-boards many belfries have Rules of Conduct, some of these also extremely ancient. Even before organised ringing was established there had been some attempt to control behaviour in the belfry, mostly with the practical object of avoiding accidents. At Southill in Bedfordshire the following notice appears:

> He that wears Spur, or Hat, or Cap, or breaks a stay,
> Or from the floor does by a bellrope sway,
> Or leaves His rope down Carless on the floor,
> Or nuisance makes within the belfry Door,
> Shall sixpence forfeit for each single Crime,
> 'Twill make him carefull at another Time.

Often the penalty for bad behaviour in the belfry was exacted in beer, for this was the common form of currency for the payment of ringers. In the belfry of the parish church at Pitminster, Somerset, there was a notice which read:

> If any one do ware his hat
> When he is ringing here
> He straitte way then shall sixpence pay
> In Sider or in Bere.

One of the oldest sets of rules is to be found in the belfry of the Dartmoor village of Drewsteignton. Dating from 1694, it ends:

> Who will not to these rules agree
> Shall not belong to this belfrie
> John Hole, churchwarden

There were also compensations for good ringing. Some churches still have examples of the ringers' 'jugs' that were at one time found in most belfries. These jugs had a capacity of between two and three gallons, and in some villages were carried from house to house after ringing for refilling by local residents! They were usually inscribed indicating the donor and in some instances the names of the ringers at the time; Lincoln cathedral has a curious leather 'ringers' jack' presented by Alderman Bullen in 1782. Occasionally a note of warning was included in the inscription, for the ringing of complicated methods is not made easier by the ingestion of several pints of strong ale. One of the pleasantest and most pertinent of these admonitions is found on a ringers' jug at Beccles, Suffolk, dated 1827:

> When I am filled with liquor strong
> Each man drink once, and then ding dong.
> Drink not too much to Cloud your knobbs
> Lest you forget to make the bobbs.

The heavy consumption of beer or cider was no doubt the reason why some belfries carried a warning against 'untrussing on the leads' outside the tower on the church roof! In at least one belfry the matter was brought to the attention of ringers in terms that nobody could misinterpret; the ringers of Brington, Northamptonshire, were warned:

> . . . any one caught pissing here
> shall fourpence pay and then be clear

It is not only on belfry-boards that ringers are commemorated. Ripon cathedral has a stained glass window in the belfry recording the ringing of a peal in 1886 as part of the city's celebration on the thousandth anniversary of its charter. And at St Albans there is a beautiful modern stained glass window showing members of the band ringing a peal of Plain Bob in August 1945 to celebrate the end of the World War II. The window was designed by Martin Webb, himself a St Albans' ringer.

# CHURCH OF
# S. ANDREWS & S. BARTHOLEMEW
## ✠ ASHLEWORTH ✠
## Belfry Rules.

**1.** The bells are holy instruments dedicated to the worship of God, and must always be used for His glory.

**2.** The ringers obtain a part in the sacred minstry of God's Church, and must conduct themselves always as His ministers should do.

**3.** Every ringer must attend throughout any service for which he may come to ring and take his part with seemly behaviour and devotion.

**4.** Drinking, smoking, loud and boisterous talking or jesting, and above all disputing, are most unseemly amongst Gods ministers in His house and are strictly forbidden in this belfry.

**5.** The control of the belfry belongs by law absolutely to the Rector, and the bells may only be used by such persons, at such times, and in such manner, as he may from time to time appoint.

*Page 71*    Ringers' Rules in the ringing chamber at Ashleworth, Glos. Note the rule that every ringer must attend divine service (c 1845)

(*left*) A stage in the preparation of the core which will eventual determine the inside shape of the bell; (*below*) making the outside mould or 'cope'

## Ringing Accidents

Today warnings and admonitions to ringers to behave in a decorous manner are rarely required. But warning still must be given on the dangers that exist for inexperienced visitors to a belfry. In many churches the bells are left 'up' between services in order to avoid the lengthy and often noisy process of raising them before ringing can begin. In this position, standing upside down and resting against the slider, it takes very little to tip the bell over. It is therefore customary to lock the belfry door when the bells are up and to place a warning notice where it can easily be seen. An additional sign for the initiated is that the bellropes are tied up and looped on themselves instead of being left to trail on the floor.

When the bells are up it is a cardinal rule that no one must be allowed into the bell-chamber, for it is here that real danger exists. Most fatal accidents in belfries have been caused by the accidental touching of a bell when set, for even the slightest push, or even a footfall, can turn the bell over and crush the person beneath. Many incumbents do not appreciate this, and in Wiltshire a tragedy occurred when a parish priest decided to take the Sunday-school class on a visit to the belfry. Unfortunately the tenor bell, weighing over a ton, turned over while he was underneath it, and he was killed. Not only non-ringers are liable to such accidents, for familiarity breeds contempt and several accidents have occurred when those engaged in maintenance have decided to take the risk and adjust the bell-gear when the bells were standing.

Before any ringing starts the wise tower-captain will ensure that every ringer is accounted for, and that nobody has decided to embark on a tour of inspection of the bells unbeknown to the rest of the band. At Great Linford, Buckinghamshire, the sight of blood spiralling down a bellrope was the first indication that a check had not been made in time, and at Stoke-on-Trent a ringer was crushed to death while oiling the bearings of the

E

tenor bell, which turned over on him. Maintenance of the bells is important, of course, and neglect can also precipitate a calamity. One of the most terrifying sounds is the sudden rumble and roar from above when a clapper comes away from its bell, and there have been instances when the clapper has penetrated the floor of the belfry and appeared in a shower of plaster through the roof of the ringing-chamber. More dangerous, though less apparent, is the effect of the breaking of a stay when the bell is allowed to hit it too hard. The bell swings right over, and then back and forth, while the rope in the chamber below thrashes round the room in a truly terrifying manner. Being completely out of control, and also rising and falling with the bell, the rope can easily loop itself round an arm or leg and cause serious injury.

Apart from ringing for Sunday services the most common function for which the bells are required is for weddings. This is also the only occasion on which the ringers are paid for their services, a fact which makes it comparatively easy to assemble a band. In most towers the ringers keep only part of their fee, the remainder going into the general belfry fund where it is used for items such as cleaning materials and the provision of new ropes. Bells are frequently required at funerals particularly if the deceased is a well-known figure in the area, and in such cases they are usually rung half-muffled. This consists of placing a leather cover on one side of the clapper, though, more rarely, the whole clapper may be covered this way. There is a good deal of folklore connected with ringing for the dead and in 1702 the Rules of the London Scholars ended with a paragraph that gave instructions for the ringing of 'a Funeral or Dead Peal'. The custom was to toll the tenor bell before the funeral: nine times for a man, six times for a woman and three times for a child. A muffled peal would be rung during the service, and the bell tolled again during burial the same number of times as the years of the deceased. Until the beginning of this century it was also the custom in some rural areas to toll the passing bell when a parishioner was dying. It is to this that

John Donne's famous phrase 'for whom the bell tolls' refers, though the sound of the passing bell could hardly have improved the morale of those unfortunate enough to appreciate its significance.

The tenor bell used for funerals and for indicating the age of the dead person was called the 'teller', a name corrupted to 'tailor'. A much later writer than Donne, Dorothy Sayers, has immortalised this name in her fascinating murder story *The Nine Tailors*, in which the victim is done to death by being locked in with the bells while a peal is being rung. For a person who was not a ringer Miss Sayers performed the amazing feat of describing accurately and with a wealth of detail the lore of ringing. While she cannot be faulted on this score the medical aspect of the tale is less accurate; madness might well be induced by enforced contact with ringing bells, and possibly the eardrums would be fractured, but death would certainly not result. All the same, *The Nine Tailors* remains one of the finest pieces of detective fiction ever written, and is a 'must' for every potential ringer.

One of the least-known aspects of ringing is the annual outing which is traditional in most belfries. Ringers generally have little opportunity to ring in other towers and therefore one day a year is set aside for this purpose. A coach is hired and the ringers, usually accompanied by wives, friends and other non-ringers, set out for a tour of churches, perhaps many miles away. The outing is normally held on a Saturday in summer and in most towers is the high-spot of the ringing-year. A great deal of preparation is required beforehand. The organiser must first decide the area in which the outing is to take place and how long it will take to get there before the first bells can be rung. Suitable towers must then be selected, usually a total of about six or seven, and the incumbent approached for permission to ring on that day. An outing is a most enjoyable experience, for ringers and non-ringers alike, and the journey homeward at the end of the day is frequently enlivened by ringing on handbells, usually brought on the outing, making a pleasant change from the somewhat bibulous rendering of 'Nellie Dean' which is so often the mark of the returning coach party in England.

Ringing in towers other than his own is an important experience for the learner. He compares the feel of other bells, the sights and sounds of new ringing chambers and the exchange of ideas and aids to better ringing. He can do this, of course, apart from the annual outing, either by going to a nearby tower occasionally for Sunday ringing or by joining the ringers on their practice night. Some experienced ringers indulge in what is known as 'tower-grabbing'. This pernicious pastime consists of sallying forth at weekends or at holiday periods to distant towers and attempting to ring. Sometimes permission is not even requested, and on entering the church the 'grabbers' immediately take the ropes and begin ringing. This is not only the negation of civilised behaviour, but in many cases has resulted in damage to bell-gear that was not in a fit state for ringing.

To the untrained ear, one of the pleasantest experiences is listening to a striking competition. This is a feature found mainly in the west of England, where prowess in method-ringing is not given the inflated importance it enjoys in London and in other parts. Those who complain of the 'noise' of the bells should listen to a striking competition. The regular rhythm, the steady stroke, the same sequence repeated several times before a change is made, all help convey the true beauty of bellringing. And, of course, there is the competitive element, with loyalties aroused and much sagacious head-wagging on the part of the experts listening outside. It is part of a very long tradition, older even than Stedman and all he stands for. Good striking is the essence of good ringing, and nowhere is it done more superbly than in the towers of Somerset, Devon and Cornwall.

# CHAPTER 8

# THE BELL-FOUNDRY

## *Bell-founders*

Among several crafts and skills lost during the Dark Ages was that of bell-founding. It had been known for centuries by the ancients, but in Britain was not revived or rediscovered until the tenth century, when we read of bells made by St Dunstan. Just over a century later, a ring of seven cast for Croyland Abbey, Lincolnshire, marks the earliest known example of a set of bells cast and tuned as a complete ring.

Medieval bell-founding in England was carried on mainly by itinerant founders who, travelling from place to place, cast new bells or repaired old ones, and established their mobile foundries as near to the church as possible. There they set up their furnaces and dug the pits in which the bells would be cast, frequently working single-handed or with an apprentice to whom they handed down the secrets of the art.

As archaeological excavations continue up and down the country sites of old foundries and bell-pits are occasionally unearthed. A recent find of great interest was at Exeter, where in 1970 the church of St Mary Major, near the cathedral, was demolished and a pit was uncovered in which was cast the bell for the Norman tower built in 1150. Though the bell itself has long disappeared, its size and probable weight can be ascertained from the shape of the brick base and mould remaining.

Whilst various combinations of metals have been used to provide the basic material for the bell, including gold, silver and zinc, the standard alloy for centuries has been a mixture of 77 per cent copper and 23 per cent tin, giving bronze.

Early bell-founders experienced difficulties in prolonging the life of the bell, for it was very likely to crack at an early stage due to constant hitting by the clapper on the same spot. To give additional strength the bell was thickened at its lip, and this was found to afford a deeper and more resonant tone. The very earliest bells surviving in Britain are tall and narrow, but with the coming of change-ringing and attempts to improve the bell's sound a new shape evolved, one of concave sides and wide mouth familiar today. With the improvement in roads and communications generally the itinerant bell-founders tended to establish their workshops and foundries on permanent sites, usually in the larger cathedral cities and in towns where churches were numerous, and, following medieval practice, as members of the same trade they tended to set up shop together in the same area. Culver Street in Salisbury, Wiltshire, was once known as 'the bell-founders' street', and in many towns and large villages one may still find a Foundry Lane close to the parish church.

At the time of the Reformation bell-founding virtually ceased. Its revival during the second half of the sixteenth century may have been due to Queen Elizabeth's fear of impending invasion from the continent, and the sudden realisation that the age-old method of warning by 'firing' the bells might be impaired after the ravages perpetrated by her father. At all events the art of bell-founding expanded and flourished during the years that followed, assisted greatly by the awakened interest in change-ringing created by Fabian Stedman. Bells made from this period onwards were often inscribed with the founder's name or mark (prior to that the name inscribed, if any, was more likely to be that of the donor) enabling us to identify the most prolific founders of their day and the areas in which they worked. Miles Graye was established in Colchester in

1605 and Christopher Hodson of London recast Oxford's 'Great Tom' in 1681.

One of the best known bell-founding families were the Rudhalls of Gloucester who were in business from 1684 to about 1830, and whose many famous bells include the ring at St Martins-in-the-Fields in London. In Somerset the Purdue and Bilbie families were famous, as were the Penningtons of Devon. Thomas Bilbie was such a perfectionist that in 1750 he killed himself after failing to tune a bell accurately. For close on 200 years, until about 1740, the Knight family at Reading cast church bells almost without stop; about 300 bells from this famous foundry still exist. From 1506 the Newcombe family was established at Leicester where they cast bells for over a century. It was rivalled only by the Watts family, in the same city, who were at work from 1563 to 1637, and they opened another foundry at Bedford about 1590.

In London a certain Robert Mot established himself in business as a bell-founder in 1570, with premises just off the Whitechapel Road. It is possible he came from Canterbury, where his father John Mot was known to have built up a successful scrap-metal business from the plunder of the monasteries and churches at the time of the Dissolution. It may be because of Mot's association with the district that many of his bells are found in Kent, though his activities were not confined to the manufacture of bells. By 1588 he was casting cannon for use against the Armada, and at the same time providing bells for Westminster Abbey.

Since then the Whitechapel foundry has had several owners, from the Bartletts, who followed Carter, through the Lester and Pack families, Pack and Chapman, Chapman and Mears, and Mears and Stainbank, to the present day, when it is in the hands of William and Douglas Hughes. Since 1570 the foundry has been in continuous production, though it changed to new premises in the Whitechapel Road in 1738, on the site of the old Artichoke Inn. Over the years it acquired several other famous foundries, closing them down and transferring production to Whitechapel; among them were the Gloucester foundry of the Rudhalls, that of Robert Wells of Aldbourne, Wiltshire, Osborn & Dobson of Downham Market, Norfolk, and the well-known foundry of John Briant at Hertford.

During this extraordinary 400-year period of continuous output the Whitechapel foundry has been responsible for many famous bells. At home its most publicised achievement was the casting of Big Ben in 1858 after the unfortunate first attempt by Warner & Company of Cripplegate. Understandably, many of the City of London churches have bells by the Whitechapel foundry, including the famous Bow Bells of St Mary-le-Bow, Cheapside, the 'Oranges and Lemons' bells of St Clement Danes, and the bells of St Michael's, Cornhill, St Olave's, Hart Street and St Leonard's, Shoreditch.

The Whitechapel foundry was sending bells abroad by the middle of the eighteenth century, and inherited responsibility for the famous Liberty Bell of the USA cast by Rudhalls of Gloucester in 1752. The bell cracked and was recast by Pass & Stowe of Philadelphia and later proclaimed the Declaration of Independence on 4 July 1776. It cracked again in 1835 when tolling the death of Chief Justice Marshall, but like Big Ben in London it has not been recast and remains cracked to this day. In 1970 the president of an organisation called the Procrastinators of America visited the Whitechapel Bell Foundry to lodge an official complaint about the crack in the Liberty Bell! The complaint was noted, though the blame was attributed to the faulty workmanship of the original American bell-hangers. Despite this 'complaint', the Whitechapel foundry appears not to have lost a customer, for it is currently engaged in casting 2,400 replicas of the Liberty Bell for sale in the USA to celebrate the bi-centenary of the Declaration of Independence in 1976.

The oldest ring of American bells actually cast at Whitechapel is that at Christ Church, Philadelphia, dating from 1754. Another famous American import from the Whitechapel Road is the ring of eight bells in the church of St Michael, Charleston, South Carolina. These bells were seized by the British during the War of Independence and taken back to England. After the war they were redeemed by an American merchant and returned to St Michael's. On the outbreak of the Civil War they went to Columbia, South Carolina, for safe keeping but unfortunately disintegrated when that city was destroyed by fire in 1865. The broken pieces were recovered, however, and later sent back to the Whitechapel foundry for recasting into the modern bells that hang in the church today. In latter years the most impressive export of the Whitechapel Bell Foundry has been the ring of ten at Washington Cathedral.

Today the Whitechapel foundry is still in business in the same street where it has existed for 400 years, and is busier than ever. But another move seems imminent, for this area of London's East End is being developed and though the attractive frontage of 1739 is scheduled as a building of historical interest the planners do not envisage a continuance of foundry work on the premises to the rear and adjoining. It will be a sad severance of a connection with Whitechapel that has lasted since 1570, but it is reasonably certain that production will not be allowed to halt during the move, even if it is restricted only to the casting of the Liberty Bell replicas.

The Industrial Revolution in England caused the demise of many famous bell-foundries as workers turned to less exacting and better paid employment in other branches of engineering. Some smaller foundries survived well into the twentieth century, as, for example, that of the famous Oxfordshire founder, Henry Bond, at Burford. Indeed, a new bell-founding enterprise started as late as 1877 when Arthur Johnson became partner in the clockmaking firm established by William Gillett at Croydon, Surrey, in 1844. This firm made rapid strides, and introduced improved methods of casting and tuning so that contracts were obtained not only for English church bells but for carillons and chimes for Europe, the United States and the Commonwealth. The foundry was responsible for producing the world's largest carillon (74 bells) at Riverside Drive

Church, New York, and carillons at Parliament Buildings in Ottawa, Princeton University, and the New Zealand War Memorial at Wellington. Gillett and Johnston continued bell-founding until 1957 when they were taken over by a group of engineering companies and from then onwards reverted to clock-making only. It is pleasant to record that in 1965 the company left the group and is today once again privately owned. The Whitechapel foundry is not alone in the field. There is one other, well away from London—the Taylor bell-foundry at Loughborough in Leicestershire. This foundry, though claiming a tenuous connection with the old Leicester foundry, really began with Robert Taylor at St Neots in 1782 when Robert ended his apprenticeship to Edward Arnold, a bell-founder of Leicester. Robert appears to have made an almost instant success of his calling, and his bells are found throughout the Midlands and the Eastern Counties. In 1821, after the St Neots premises had been destroyed by fire, Robert Taylor moved to Oxford with his family, and there he died in 1830 and was buried in the churchyard of St Ebbe's (his grave is not marked). His youngest son, John, who with his elder brother had helped to run the Oxford foundry, had already branched out on his own and gone to Devon to set up a foundry. Eight years after his father's death he returned to Oxford, but the renewal of association with his brother did not last long and very soon he had left for Loughborough, where he had been commissioned to recast the bells of the parish church. Finding Loughborough to his liking he remained, and in 1859 brought a plot of ground in what was then a cherry orchard and built the premises we see today. Furthermore, the Taylor family are still in control and Mr Paul Taylor who runs the firm at present is a direct descendant of the original Robert Taylor whose apprenticeship ended in 1782. Though the history of Taylor's foundry is shorter, and certainly less static, than that of Whitechapel, the foundry has been in the hands of one family far longer than has the London enterprise. Two hundred years of continuity have enabled the Taylor foundry to contribute greatly to the improvement of techniques of bell-founding.

The Loughborough foundry, set amid narrow streets of red-brick early Victorian houses is distinguished visually by its famous bell-tower rising above the huddled roofs. Next to the foundry, in true Victorian fashion, stands the house occupied by John Taylor, connected to the main building by a series of Dickensian passages and offices. The foundry itself is a fascinating place. Everywhere there are bells—from the sixteenth century to the twentieth—piled on each other, standing in rows, each marked in chalk with the name of its church. Many are in for repair, mostly to the headstock where years of constant ringing have created a weakness that might eventually separate the bell from its moorings and bring it crashing down. Others are in for quarter-turning or for re-turning, while some bells, cracked beyond repair, are there to be melted down and added to bell metal for recasting into new bells. For a bell does not always die when its tour of duty ends: its metal goes into a new bell, and life begins again after two centuries or more.

## Inside the Foundry

One's first impression in a bell-foundry is of surprise that so much is still done manually in a business that is in fact a highly specialised engineering enterprise. It is one of the few crafts still to survive in modern times—even the composition of the bell-metal has changed little during the centuries. Early bell-founders had the romantic notion that precious metals such as gold and silver would improve the quality of the sound, but unfortunately this is not so. Gold, even if it were economically possible to use it, would produce a sound equivalent to that of a bell made of lead! This being so the standard 'mix' of approximately 13 parts of copper to 4 parts of tin is used, the metal being brought to the required melting point in furnaces ranged round the foundry walls. The total capacity of bell-metal available from the furnaces at Loughborough is about 25 tons, and the metal is 'tapped' ready for pouring into the mould when at a bright orange heat of about 1,100° C.

The mould into which the metal is poured is itself a complex piece of equipment made with the greatest care and skill. A base-plate is first prepared, slightly larger than the diameter of the mouth of the bell, and then an inside and an outside mould. The inside mould is built up round a conical pile of bricks and consists of sand, clay, chopped straw and manure. Next, the outside mould or cope is made, using a cast-iron case on the inside of which a similar mixture of loam is built up. This moulds the exterior of the bell, and, like the surface of the inner core, must be perfectly smooth and of accurate contour. The core and cope are dried in oil-fired ovens until hard enough to be used.

When ready they are removed from the oven and the cope is fitted over the core, rather like one flower-pot over another, the space between representing the shape of the eventual bell. Clamped in this position, with an orifice left at the top of the cope, the dual mould is lowered into a specially prepared pit of sand in the foundry floor until about a third of it is below floor level. When the bell-metal is ready in the furnace, casting starts, the molten metal being swung in a crucible across from the oven to the mould and carefully tipped into the hole at the top of the cope. This continues until the space between cope and core is filled, the metal round the orifice being constantly stirred to prevent its solidifying and so blocking the aperture. It is then left to cool. With bells up to about a ton the mass of metal in the mould will have cooled sufficiently in a day for the cope to be lifted off and the bell examined, though heavier bells may need almost a week before this is possible. The bell is then lifted off the core, the inside carefully examined, and then transferred to another part of the foundry for the arduous exercise of accurate tuning. While the cope was being made the inscription and symbols to appear on the outside of the bell were put on it by means of letters made from box-wood.

The art of bell-tuning had been practised on the continent

long before it became familiar in this country. Even so it was
not until the seventeenth century that the Hemony family,
bell-founders in the Netherlands, analysed the actual series
of notes produced by a bell and attempted to match them
accurately. A bell, when struck, gives out not just one note
but a series of them. They can be identified and occur at
definite musical intervals. In a bell giving out a main note of
C the additional notes heard are as illustrated musically below:

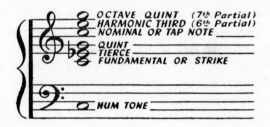

The main note heard is called the fundamental, or strike
note, while the nominal is heard an octave above and the hum
note an octave below—the latter taking its name from the
hum that continues, with most bells, long after the other
sounds have died away. In between are other notes, the main
ones being a minor third called the 'tierce' and the fifth, or
'quint'. All these extra notes are known as 'partials'. When
the bell is struck the whole of the metal mass vibrates, from
crown to lip, the higher parts producing the higher notes and
the lower part, at the lip, producing the hum note. The more
metal present the deeper the note. While the presence of the
additional notes, notably the tierce, may be desirable they
must not be allowed to intrude on the main note required for
the bell. The art of the bell tuner is to remove excess metal
from the parts of the bell producing these additional notes,
at the same time keeping the relationship, or interval, between
the notes accurate.

Early bell-founders attempted to achieve this by chipping
away excess metal with a chisel, but today a different pro-

cedure is adopted. The bell is inverted on a special stand, and a fast-moving lathe skims off the metal round the inside of the bell over the desired area. In a small bell this is a most delicate operation, as the area of metal producing any given note may be only a fraction of an inch. In a large bell it may be as much as 6in, but its proportion to the whole surface remains the same and absolute accuracy is essential. The tuner must have an extremely accurate ear (perfect pitch is a great help, though comparatively rare) as once the metal has been removed and the note altered there is no way of replacing it. To allow for this most bells are cast to produce a sound a tone lighter than is desired, and each part of the bell scraped until the tone is lowered to the desired pitch. A bell which is cast to produce the correct note without further tuning is called a 'maiden' bell. When finished, the bell is a silver-grey externally, but once hung in a tower it quickly turns to the more familiar grey-green colour induced by the elements.

Before the bell leaves the foundry all the associated 'gear' must be made, including the all-important clapper. This, too, is produced with care and mathematical accuracy, for the swing of the clapper and its weight have a definite effect not only on the sound of the bell but on its future life. Victorian and earlier bell-founders tended to equate a heavy clapper with a sonorous note, hence the unfortunate affair of the crack in Big Ben, the Liberty Bell and several others. The clapper was formerly made of wrought-iron, but in the absence of this metal in modern engineering steel is now used, though it is not as satisfactory as wrought-iron because of its tendency to break. Also cast at the foundry are the headstocks for the bells as well as the massive iron frames which support them in the belfry. In the carpenter's shop the wheels are made on which the bells are mounted, part oak and part ash, and at the end of the process the complete bell is mounted on a special ringing machine and tested thoroughly.

With only two bell-foundries left in England, and increasing demand from overseas in addition to home orders, it is not surprising that the industry seems set for a bright future. At present an order from either foundry takes from nine to twelve months to execute. The problem is not so much one of capacity but of personnel, for a craft such as this takes many years to acquire, and, in the words of Paul Taylor, 'how many school-leavers want to become bell-founders?' Bell-founders elsewhere are scarce too—there are less than twenty in Europe, mainly in Belgium, Germany and France. These firms rarely cast bells for the kind of full-circle ringing done in Britain but concentrate almost entirely on bells for carillons. So the Loughborough and Whitechapel foundries continue to meet heavy demands, producing new rings and repairing and recasting old ones. It would be tragic indeed if they were to close down through lack of manpower.

## Hanging the Bells

From the foundry the bells travel to the church, where they often remain on view for several days before being hauled up into the belfry through the trapdoor in the floor of the ringing chamber. In more spacious days the arrival of new bells was attended with great jollification and the ceremony of dedication was performed by the incumbent before an admiring crowd of villagers. But before the cleric had a chance to bless the bells they were often given what Dr Alfred Gatty in 1847 called 'a profane christening'. The smallest bell was inverted and filled with a mixture of ale, rum, porter and any other drink which happened to be at hand or expendable, and doled out to the audience free of charge. Says Dr Gatty: 'The Bell Founder's representative is busy on this occasion, and another bell has a more delicate mixture from which he offers a libation to the more distinguished of the company.' The merrymaking associated with new bells goes back at least to the early eighteenth century, for in 1745 that amiable and gentle cleric, Gilbert White, described the arrival of the recast ring of bells at his village church of Selborne: 'The day of the arrival of this tuneable peal was observed as a high festival by the village, and rendered more joyous by an order from the donor that the treble bell should be fixed, bottom upwards in the ground, and filled with punch of which all persons were permitted to partake.'

When at last the junketing is over, the bells are solemnly blessed and a service is held at which, almost inevitably, will be sung some Victorian hymns written specially for such occasions though hardly noted for their originality or depth of feeling.

In the tower itself the bell-hangers have been at work for some days, or even weeks, repairing and strengthening the existing frame to take an augmented ring, or to ensure that the original is in perfect condition, for it is not often that the frame can be examined in the absence of the bells. Even so, installing a new frame in a tower is a skilled and arduous operation involving working in a confined space that becomes even more confined once the actual process of bell-hanging begins. Both bell-foundries in England have their own staff of experienced bell-hangers, but there are also several private individuals and small firms who carry out this work. Typical of these specialist firms, who need no publicity and, indeed, often appear to shun it, is the White family of Appleton, Berkshire, just across the Thames from Oxford. Here Frank White carries on the tradition established by his great grandfather Alfred White in the reign of George IV. The Whites are famous bell-hangers but their skills do not end there. In the workshops at Appleton are made the timber frames for the bells, the wooden wheels on which they are mounted, together with much other bell-gear. Until comparatively recently they also cast handbells and still supply them, though now they buy in rough-cast bells from the two big foundries and tune and perfect them in their own workshops.

It was Alfred White's work, in connection with the augmentation of Appleton church bells from six to eight in 1854, that made the village a centre for ringing and established the tradition of 'March the Fourth'. This is a ringing festival held on

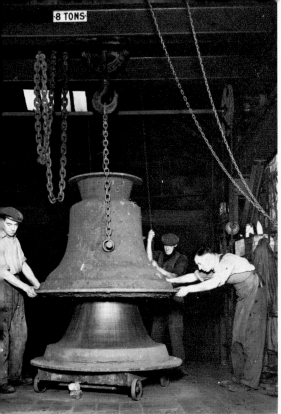

Page 89
(*left*) The cope being lowered over the core preparatory to casting; (*below*) molten bell metal being poured into the two halves of the mould to cast the bell

(*left*) Model showing the construction of bell, wheel, rope and frame. The bell is 'down'

(*right*) As above. In this photograph the bell is 'up' at hand-stroke

the nearest Saturday to 4 March each year (the anniversary of the installation of the new ring) and attended by ringers from all over England. Activities usually begin with a peal attempt in the morning and ringing is continuous all day. Both village inns remain open, and in the evening the Appleton Ringers, formed in 1830, invite their friends to a dinner at which over a hundred may be present. Those residents of Appleton who do not care for ringing take to the hills or seek sanctuary with friends in Oxford, for attendance at an Appleton 'March the Fourth' is one occasion on which physical fitness is an asset in ringing. Alfred White himself is buried in Appleton church-yard in a grave headed by a wrought-iron representation of a ring of ten bells.

## Inscriptions

Bell inscriptions are a study in themselves and tell the historian a great deal. Medieval bell-founders were concerned with making bells that were pleasant in tone and acknowledged the gift of the bells by inscribing the name or initials of the donor. Rarely did they insert their own name, and early founders can be identified only with difficulty from the style of lettering or from a particular emblem used. Even so, successors to a founder often continued using the same emblem for many years after the original user was dead, and it was not until after the Reformation that the identity of the founder was recorded with any clarity. The Latin dedication commonly used was inscribed in ornate and flowery lettering: short words and names were often abbreviated or the initial letter only given, and longer words broken up with a cross or foliated pattern between each syllable. The words were divided from each other by stops sometimes consisting of a portrait of the reigning monarch or, with medieval humour, of grotesque faces similar to those found in the misericords of the choir in many cathedrals and abbeys.

From the eighteenth century onwards Latin inscriptions became fewer and the former custom of dedicating a bell to a

F

saint and inscribing his name on it fell into disuse. From this period, too, ornate lettering vitually ceased and Roman script was used. Nineteenth-century inscriptions are legible, often in English, and mostly uninspiring. Verses became popular, often written by the parish priest and not always in the tradition of Shakespeare. One such verse reads:

> We hang here to record
> That the church was restored
> In the Year of Our Lord
> 1858

Some of the more outspoken inscriptions on bells date from the competitive period of the early 1700s when new bells were being cast and old rehung in the enthusiastic era of early change-ringing. Subscriptions were invited for the cost of the bells, usually from the squire or other local landowner, and their generosity or otherwise is occasionally recorded for posterity in the inscription. The more money subscribed, the heavier and deeper could be the bells, which accounts for the plaintive lines on a bell in Glastonbury hung in 1776:

> Our tones would all have been much deeper
> If contributions had been greater.

Inscriptions like this are a welcome relief from the all-too-frequent 'Unto the church I doe you call—death to the grave will summon all' which appears on the tenor bell at Amersham in Buckinghamshire and, with variations, on many tenors throughout the country. The inscription on most treble bells is characteristically lighter, as on the treble of the parish church at Buckingham:

> I mean to make it understood
> That tho I'm little yet I'm good.
> 1782

Reference is often made to the fact that the treble bell is the first to ring, as at St John the Baptist, Stone: 'I as trebbl be ginn' (1726). Most cheerful of all, perhaps, is the inscription on the little treble at Northenden, Manchester: 'Here goes, my brave boys.' Enthusiasm such as this must surely communicate itself down the bellrope to the ringer below!

# CHAPTER 9

# SOME INTERESTING BELLS

Bells have their place in *The Guinness Book of Records*: for instance, the heaviest bell in the world is the Tsar Kolokol bell in Moscow, weighing 193 tons and 22ft wide at its mouth. But statistics, like all potted information of this kind, can be misleading and any appreciation of the comparative size and weight of bells is only possible if there is a clear understanding of their correct function. So far we have been discussing bells that form part of a 'ring' and can be made to sound by swinging them round in a complete circle by means of a wheel and rope. Obviously there must be a limit to the weight of a bell that can be handled this way, and in fact the heaviest bell in Britain hung for true ringing is the Emmanuel Bell of Liverpool Cathedral, weighing 4 tons 2cwt, the tenor of a ring of thirteen bells. Next heaviest for ringing is Exeter Cathedral's tenor of 3 tons 12cwt, followed by the tenor of St Paul's Cathedral ring of twelve, weighing 3 tons 2cwt. If, however, a bell is not intended to be swung round and rung in the conventional manner, but chimed or struck externally by a hammer, then its weight can be very much greater and is limited only by the capacity of the foundry in which it was cast, or by the strength of the building in which it is housed. Britain's heaviest chiming bell is Great Paul, at St Paul's Cathedral in London, which turns the scales at 16¾ tons, and has a diameter of 9ft 6in. Great Paul was cast by Taylor's of Loughborough in 1881 on instructions from the Dean and Chapter of St Paul's who, in turn, were guided largely by Dr John Stainer, organist of the cathedral and composer of the famous oratorio *The Crucifixion*. Great Paul, the biggest and heaviest bell ever cast in Britain, presented problems both in its manufacture and its subsequent transportation from Loughborough to London. There were those who forecast that such a huge bell would crack, as indeed Big Ben had cracked, and also Manchester's Town Hall bell only the year before. But all went well, and on 13 May 1882 Great Paul began its journey, on a specially constructed low-loader hauled by a steam traction engine, from the foundry to London. The journey took nearly a fortnight, and Press coverage was such that thousands turned out to watch its passage through Market Harborough, Northampton and Kettering, and even in the villages and along the country lanes the route was lined with cheering spectators. So great was the enthusiasm aroused by the monster bell that at Northampton it had to be covered by a tarpaulin when it was discovered that not only were children scrawling their names in chalk on the bell, but that one enthusiast was actually about to emboss his initials on the metal with a punch and hammer. For the rest of the journey the bell had a strong police guard. A second traction engine helped to restrain it on the steep downward slope from Highgate to Holloway, then its journey continued through Upper Street, Islington, and Aldergate Street, and at 8 pm on Sunday, 21 May 1882, the procession drew up at the south-west corner of the cathedral.

Ten days later the lifting of the bell into the tower commenced, the operation being under the control of the Royal Engineers from Woolwich Arsenal. Lifting-gear and ropes normally used to move 35 ton cannon were employed, and the bell was raised into position in the remarkably short time of fifteen hours. Once regular ringing had begun, many criticisms were voiced at the inaudibility of this great bell. Letters appeared in the Press pointing out that the bell had made more noise on its journey from Loughborough than it had made since arriving in London, and a broadsheet appeared headed: 'Great Paul Tongue-tied; Why Don't He Speak Out?' Nobody seemed to know.

Certainly there was nothing wrong with the bell itself, and if there was a fault it may have been in the hanging. Later it was mounted on a larger wheel, which enabled the bell to be swung through a wider arc, though this needed the services of at least four men. Further improvements in the hanging caused the bell to sound more loudly, but even today its range remains surprisingly limited. The best place to hear it from is across the river at Bankside where, after a silence of thirty years, its sonorous tone now produced by an electrical swinging mechanism is rich and mellow even if strangely subdued for the biggest bell in England.

Though Great Paul is the heaviest bell in the Commonwealth, there is little doubt that Big Ben is the most famous—probably the most famous bell in the world. It had already served over twenty years in the clock-tower at Westminster when Great Paul made the journey from Loughborough to London.

For many people Big Ben *is* the clock-tower at Westminster, but it is one bell only—the hour bell of the Westminster chimes. It is, of course, a big bell, weighing slightly over $13\frac{1}{2}$ tons, and was first cast in 1856 by the one-time foundry of Warners at Stockton-on-Tees. This first bell weighed nearly 16 tons, and after casting was sent by rail to West Hartlepool and from there by sea to London. From the Port of London it was pulled across Westminster Bridge on a dray drawn by sixteen white horses, and was mounted on a gallows in New Palace Yard where it became one of the sights of London. It remained on view for most of 1857, but towards the end of that year a crack 4ft long was discovered. During the year it had

been tested regularly each week, and many were the theories
to account for the sudden appearance of the flaw, the most per-
sistent being that the clapper was too heavy. Warners were
asked to re-cast the bell, which they were apparently not too
willing to do as they stipulated a price far in excess of the
original quotation.

The Whitechapel Bell Foundry eventually undertook the
work, and by April 1858 they had broken down the bell and
recast it in a slightly lighter form. In October of that year the
new bell was brought back to Westminster and hauled up into
the clock-tower, where it has remained ever since. But Big
Ben's troubles were not yet over. There were difficulties with
the clock mechanism, which proved too weak to move the
enormous hands of the clock designed by Sir Charles Barry,
architect of the Houses of Parliament. But at last everything
was working satisfactorily, and on 11 July 1859 Big Ben boomed
out the hours from Westminster for the first time. In Septem-
ber, however, Big Ben cracked again. This time the uproar
almost drowned the sound of the bells themselves. There was
controversy, there was criticism and there was legal action.
The sound of Big Ben was heard no more for the next three
years, the hour being chimed by the fourth of the quarter-bells
during this time. Finally, after consultation with the Astro-
nomer Royal, it was given a quarter-turn so that the clapper
hit a different part of the bell, and the weight of the clapper
was reduced from $6\frac{1}{2}$ cwt to 4cwt. In 1862 Big Ben went into
service again and has been at work ever since. It is still cracked,
and always will be, but this has in no way marred the affection
in which this famous bell is held the world over. Its début as
an international performer took place on New Year's Eve, 1923,
when, connected by line to the BBC studios in Savoy Hill,
just off the Strand, Big Ben first broadcast to the world.

Though not altogether pertinent to the subject of bells and
bellringing some of the facts and figures associated with Big
Ben and its clock are of interest. The name of Big Ben is
popularly supposed to be derived from that of the then Com-

missioner of Works, the enormously fat Sir Benjamin Hall. This may be so, but *The Times* had been alluding to 'Big Ben of Westminster' long before the debate in Parliament at which the name was supposedly first used in 1857, and it is more likely that it was taken from another 'Big Ben', a prize-fighter of the time who had achieved notoriety by lasting sixty rounds in a drawn fight with Bendigo in 1856. The fighting Big Ben, whose real name was Benjamin Caunt, weighed over 17 stone and, like the bell itself, was the heaviest in his class.

The concept of Big Ben cannot be attributed to any one man, but the prime mover in the matter was undoubtedly E. B. Denison, the future Baron Grimthorpe. Denison was a lawyer and an amateur 'expert' on almost every conceivable subject including bells and clocks. Working with E. J. Dent, who was already well known as a maker of marine chronometers, Denison devised a completely new form of gravity escapement for the Westminster clock and this has since been adopted for most large tower-clocks throughout the world. Denison and Dent had previously collaborated in a prize-winning clock shown at the Great Exhibition of 1851 which is now to be seen above King's Cross station, built the following year.

The Westminster clock-tower housing Big Ben rises 316ft from the level of the Thames and there are 336 stairs to the belfry. Each face of the clock is 23ft in diameter, the minute spaces are 1ft apart and the figures 2ft long. An unusual feature is the use of the roman IV instead of the more common IIII. The hour hands on each face are 9ft long and the minute hands 14ft. Big Ben itself is 9ft wide at its mouth, and the notorious crack in the bell is still plainly visible.

Outside London the two heaviest bells hung for chiming are Great George at Liverpool Cathedral (nearly 15 tons) and York Minster's Great Peter of close on 11 tons. York Minster also has a famous ring of twelve with a 3 ton tenor. These bells, or rather the absence of their sound, caused some controversy early in 1972 when it was found that there were not enough ringers to ring in the New Year—the year of the 500th anniversary of the completion of the Minster in 1472 and also the year of the completion of the £2 million restoration scheme begun in 1967. The truth of the matter was that, despite the protestations of the traditionalists, ringing in the New Year had been stopped by the York police as far back as 1936 owing to rowdyism in the precincts of the minster. By the time the police had agreed to lift the ban in December 1971, and the dean and chapter had reluctantly given their consent, there was only a week left to find the ringers. York, like many other cities, depends to a large degree on ringers from the university, none of whom are available during the holiday period.

It is a comment on the general attitude to ringing that though the citizens of York were highly incensed at the absence of ringers on this occasion, only a very few have expressed any interest in the bells or shown any desire to become ringers themselves. Admittedly the bells of York Minster are notoriously 'difficult' and it is virtually impossible to teach a beginner on them, but there are several towers in the area where tuition can be undertaken. However, a peal was achieved on the minster bells during the Thanksgiving Celebrations in July of that year, and several quarter-peals were rung by the Yorkshire Association in other towers including Handsworth, Huntington, Wentworth, Rotherham and Selby Abbey.

Further south a celebrated bell is Great Tom at Christchurch, Oxford, a 6 ton performer whose voice is still heard 101 times each evening calling home the original number of undergraduates. Such a lengthy and frustrating exercise took, one might say, its toll, and Great Tom was cracked and recast at least six times during the eighteenth century. Oxford, of course, is a ringer's paradise for there never was such a place for ringing, and almost every tower is famous. With a dozen towers within the city limits and six or so immediately outside it is no surprise that Oxford supports both a flourishing society of university ringers, an active town association, and a diocesan guild. Cambridge is less fortunate in having only seven ringable towers including those at Chesterton, Trumpington and

Cherry Hinton, but has fame enough in having at its centre the ancient church of St Benedict, where Fabian Stedman himself was a ringer.

Though East Anglia is considered the cradle of ringing in England it is notable that at neither of its great cathedrals at Ely and Norwich is there a ringable peal of bells. Peterborough Cathedral has a ring of five—the heaviest in the world, and at Boston the famous 'Stump'—the church of St Botolph—has a ring of ten housed just above an enormous ringing chamber. In addition the church has fifteen more bells hung for chiming.

In London the most famous bells after St Paul's are probably those of Westminster Abbey, augmented in November 1971 from a ring of eight to a ring of ten by the addition of two new trebles from the Whitechapel bell-foundry. The dedication of the new ring was performed in the presence of Her Majesty the Queen in the Abbey, the bells standing on the floor of the nave preparatory to being hauled aloft. Shortly before the service an elderly lady, seeing the great bells standing on the floor, inquired how often they were taken down for dusting!

Yet it is not the grandeur of Westminster or the majesty of St Paul's that captures the popular imagination when bells are thought of, but the churches of the City of London.

St Clement Danes, on its island site in the Strand, had been represented by a church for nearly seven hundred years when it was finally decided to demolish it. Sir Christopher Wren's superb new building of St Clement Danes was erected in 1682; eleven years later 'eight noble bells' were cast and hung in the tower and forty years after that, in February 1733, the first full peal was rung on them by the College Youths. In 1843 the ring was increased to ten and for the next hundred years St Clement Danes was one of the most popular ringing towers in the metropolis. At the beginning of World War II the bells were taken down for safety and housed in the base of the tower, but one night in May 1941, when all London seemed ablaze, this noble church was gutted by incendiary bombs, only tower and walls remaining. The bells, red-hot in the inferno and then swamped by water from the fire hoses, were cracked beyond repair. St Clement Danes was restored in 1955 by the Royal Air Force as a memorial to the Commonwealth airmen who lost their lives in the war. The bells were recast and rehung by the Whitechapel bell-foundry and have been rung regularly for Sunday service since 1958. There is also a carillon attachment provided to enable 'Oranges and Lemons' to be played.

St Michael's, Cornhill, another famous City church, was completely gutted in the Great Fire of London in 1666. It was already famous for its bells, for John Stow, the great historian of London, said of them: 'This was accounted the best ring of six bells that was to be rung by six men that was in England, for harmony, sweetness of sound and tune.' After the fire the new church, again designed by Wren, had to wait until 1728 for its new bells, but when they were at last provided they proved to be a minor wonder—one of the first rings of twelve ever installed. For this reason they attracted the 'scientific' ringers of the Exercise, and many notable peals were scored, particularly after 1910 when the bells were lowered one stage in the tower and ringing became easier. Curiously, St Michael's escaped major damage in the war, though a minor fire in the ringing chamber destroyed most of the historic peal-boards housed there.

St Bartholomew the Great in Smithfield was founded by Rahere, the court jester, in 1123. As it was part of a priory it fell victim to the Reformation; most of the building that stands today dates from about 1630. Despite all this it has the oldest complete ring of five bells in existence. It is a light ring, with a tenor of only 5½cwt, and the cost of installing the bells appears in the churchwardens' accounts for 1510.

The famous Bow Bells are the twelve bells of St Mary-le-Bow, Cheapside, another Wren church rebuilt since the end of World War II. Only seven years before the outbreak of hostilities the bells had been in poor condition and had been restored mainly through the generosity of Gordon Selfridge. Over the river at Southwark the cathedral church of St Saviour has the heaviest ringing bell in London after St Paul's (48cwt).

Outside London there are many notable rings and bells, each famous on account of age, weight or some unusual factor in their history. Wells Cathedral has the heaviest ring of ten in existence, while Beverley Minster in Yorkshire has a modern ring of ten by Taylor's of Loughborough in one tower and the famous Great John weighing 7 tons, and from the same foundry, in its other tower. There is regular ringing on the ten, and for the hour chimes the quarters are rung on part of the ring. This arrangement at Beverley is probably the only example in existence of one clock-mechanism striking bells in two separate towers.

Donations of single bells by private individuals are relatively common, but it is rare for a complete ring to be provided in this way. At Port Sunlight in Cheshire, the village church which is undenominational has a ring of eight donated in 1906 by William Lever, the first Lord Leverhulme, and in 1921 a South Wales nonconformist, J. Morgan gave a ring of eight bells to the parish church of Llanfigan.

One of the most interesting but lesser known rings privately subscribed is that in the Queen's Tower of what was formerly the Imperial Institute in South Kensington, already mentioned under secular towers (page 63). It could equally well be classified under 'detached towers' for the former buildings of the Imperial Institute adjoining it have been swept away and a new building, now named Imperial College, erected on another site near-by. The Imperial Institute was built to commemorate Queen Victoria's Golden Jubilee in 1887, and was intended to foster commercial and scientific progress throughout what was then the British Empire, and to house exhibits from the colonies demonstrating this progress. The building included a lofty tower and was opened by Queen Victoria in May 1893. The tower had no bells, and was probably not designed to have any, but in 1893, the year of the opening of the Institute, a wealthy

Australian lady, Mrs Elizabeth Millar, then living at Kew, offered to pay for the casting and installation of a ring of ten bells. The offer was gratefully accepted, and as a mark of gratitude the eighty-three-year-old Mrs Millar was offered honorary membership of the Society of College Youths, which she gracefully declined. The bells themselves are a very fine ring cast by Taylor's of Loughborough, with a 38cwt tenor. Each bell carries an inscription:

> Elizabeth Millar gave me—
> The Loughborough Taylors made me

and they are named, from treble to tenor: Maud, Victoria, Louise, George, Albert Victor, Arthur, Alfred, Alexandra, Albert Edward and Victoria RI.

Unfortunately the bells are hung near the top of this 300ft tower and the sway induced by the moving mass of metal militates against good striking; this is made even more difficult by the ringing chamber being immediately underneath the bells. The problems of ringing here were apparent from the first, and at the opening ceremony the bells were in the care of John Taylor, from the family firm that had cast the bells, who was told that the ringers selected for the occasion should represent the whole of the ringing associations in the country. That Taylor actually found a representative band is greatly to his credit, and Queen Victoria is reported to have stopped her carriage on the opening day especially to listen to the bells.

But full peals have been few at the Imperial Institute. The first was to mark the Coronation of Edward VII in 1902, and the last recorded complete peal was rung by the College Youths in November 1964. From the first it was intended that the bells should be rung only on royal anniversaries and birthdays, and this has been faithfully adhered to since, with short lengths being rung about eight times a year.

Another and much better-known ring of 'royal' bells is in the Curfew Tower of Windsor Castle. The tower was built in

1230, and in a document of 1249 we read of 'four bells to be put in the Chapel of the Castle at Windsor'. The present St George's Chapel was built in 1475 and the bells moved to the new belfry three years later. The eight seventeenth-century bells that now form the ring are hung anti-clockwise and are rung on royal festivals and church feasts. But they are struck mechanically three times a day, before Holy Communion, Matins and Evensong, in a precise order which has continued through the centuries. The first bell summons the sacristan to the chapel, the second the lay clerks and the third the choir, after which the remaining five bells ring for a short time. As their sound dies away the sacristan intones the words 'Toll down' and the procession of choir and clergy move into the chapel. There is also a carillon attachment to the bells which plays the hymn tune 'St David' every three hours, after the clock has struck.

The Curfew Tower has contained many clocks in its time; the present one dates from 1689 and was installed by John Davis of Windsor. The remarkable longevity of this clock which has survived for nearly 300 years, is largely attributable to the special rust-proof alloy used by Davis in the clock parts, the secret of which died with him. Equally remarkable are the massive pale oak beams of the belfry-cage, now 500 years old; the preservative with which they were treated when they were first made has kept them continually free of woodworm.

Windsor Castle's famous Round Tower has a single bell only. It is a Russian bell cast in 1755 and called The Raven, and was brought from Sebastopol as a trophy of the Crimean War. Its harsh and anguished note is rarely heard, for it is tolled only at the death of a monarch.

Windsor parish church, along the High Street, has its own ring of eight. They are housed in the tall-pinnacled tower of Bath stone built in 1821 on the site of the 700-year-old parish church which had fallen into such disrepair that 'the performance of Divine Service within its walls was in some degree perilous'. Perhaps the ringers of Windsor were still suspicious of their new tower, or they may even have been as traditionalist as the castle itself, but for 120 years they rang nothing but call-changes, and did not attempt even a quarter-peal until March 1921. The eight bells, originally in the former church, were recast in 1715 and augmented from six to eight by Lord Marsham, Treasurer to Queen Anne, as the inscription on the bells indicates:

> I and my seven sisters were
> given by the cofferer
> And if you wish his name to know
> My elder sister you will show.

> ———

> Lord Marsham, Cofferer to Queen Anne,
> Gave these two bells and new cast
> The other six

## Iona

Windsor may have a tradition going back a thousand years, but in a remote corner of the British Isles a single bell recalls a much longer tradition, connected not with pomp and circumstance but with the simple faith of the first Christian missionaries to Britain. This bell hangs in the Abbey of Iona, on that magical island off the west coast of Scotland where 1,400 years ago St Columba landed and established a religious community. During the centuries that followed the buildings and monastery in this remote place fell into ruin, but they continued to exert an extraordinary power over the few visitors who came that way. Dr Johnson on his tour of the Highlands said, 'The man is little to be envied whose piety would not grow warmer amongst the ruins of Iona.' At the beginning of this century work began on the restoration of the abbey and its buildings, so fulfilling the prophecy attributed to Columba himself: 'Iona of my heart, Iona of my love, instead of monks' voices shall be the lowing of cattle. But before the world's end Iona shall be once more as it was.'

By 1931 the Iona community had rebuilt the abbey and in that year the foundry of John Taylor at Loughborough cast the single bell of 22cwt which hangs there today. It is hung for full ringing, though in the absence of any experienced ringer to handle it, it was chimed only at intervals for the next forty years. Early in 1971 the Warden of the community asked for advice in the proper ringing of the bell and two experienced ringers from the mainland travelled to Iona and provided the necessary tuition. A week later the full sound of this superb bell was heard for the first time calling the community to evensong. It was a dramatic and awe-inspiring moment, and it was said that the bell could be heard across the water as far away as Oban, some thirty miles distant. The inscription on the bell is a simple and appropriate one. Written in Celtic it reads 'I am Columba'. No other words are necessary.

*Page 107* The bells at Peterchurch, Herefordshire, in full swing

(*left*) Emmanuel, the tenor bell of Liverpool Cathedral, on the tuning machine at the Loughborough Bell Foundry. At 82cwt this is the heaviest bell in England hung for full-circle ringing

(*right*) The 9½ ton 'Great George' in the tower of Bristol University. Note the size of the wheel and headstock

# CHAPTER 10

# CHIMES, CARILLONS AND RINGING-MACHINES

## *Tunes from Bells*

The interest in change-ringing that was such a feature of seventeenth-century England, and the subsequent development of 'methods', did not find a parallel on the Continent of Europe. English interest in bellringing was founded mainly on the mathematical problems involved, and expertise in bell-ringing could be acquired with virtually no knowledge of music at all. On the continent, however, particularly in Flanders and the Netherlands, the standard of musicology was higher and demanded a correspondingly more melodious sound from the bells. Side by side with the spread of method-ringing in Britain there grew up, on the other side of the Channel, a tradition of bellringing that enabled recognisable tunes to be played by means of a keyboard—the chimes or carillons that are such a marked feature in Belgium and Holland today. In this technique of ringing, the bells are hung 'dead', which means that the bells themselves are not swung but the clapper is moved manually or mechanically to strike the inside of the bell. For melodies to be played the bells must be tuned chromatically and must represent at least a full octave. On eight bells, however, the number of tunes which can be played is limited, and therefore it is usual to extend the range beyond the octave and to include semi-tones. Even so, English bells tuned for normal ringing are not suitable if two or more bells are to ring in harmony, as the wrong partials predominate.

The degree of tuning needed for such ringing is of a different order from that required for change-ringing in the English system, and it is not surprising that some of the most successful carillons in Europe were made by the Hemony family, the seventeenth-century Flemish bell-founders whose researches into tuning have been mentioned earlier. Carillons of a kind had been installed before, notably in Dunkirk in as early as 1437, Alost in 1487 and Antwerp in 1540. But it was the splendid carillon made by the Hemonys for the Wine House Tower in Zutphen in 1645 that made carillons famous. Francis Hemony, the founder of the firm, died in 1667; and Peter, his son, carried on alone until 1678 when failing health caused him to close the foundry. It is interesting that the principles adopted by the Hemonys to perfect the tuning of bells were not inherited by other bell-founders, but were lost sight of until their rediscovery in England over 200 years later by a Victorian musicologist, Canon F. Simpson, whose researches were published in 1895. These principles were adopted by the Taylors in Loughborough, who built up a considerable export trade in carillons to Europe and America as a result.

The number of bells used to produce tunes decides whether the system is termed a chime or a carillon. A set of bells of less than two chromatic octaves (24 bells) is a chime, and is normally used for playing a melody in one line without accompaniment. Over this number it becomes a carillon, and the total of bells may extend to over seventy.

One of the problems of chimes and carillons is that as the bell itself does not move, but only the clapper, the volume of sound is far less than that obtained in church bellringing. Moreover, if recognised tunes are to be played there must be scope for a certain amount of expression in the playing, with the possibility of runs and arpeggios on the lighter bells in contrast to the sonorous tones of the heavier ones whose 'partial' notes may be heard longer than is required. Carillons are played from a keyboard, or clavier, the clapper of each bell being connected by a system of wires, cranks and pulleys to the appropriate wooden peg of the clavier. When the peg is depressed, by hitting with the open hand, the clapper swings against the side of the bell, producing the required note, and then swings away from it again by gravity. The problem is to equate this considerable physical effort with a lightness of touch which enables the higher-toned bells to be rung in rapid succession and in conformity with the requirements of the melodic line. Through the years many systems have been devised to achieve this objective and to provide just the correct degree of movement of the clapper with a reliability and regularity of touch on the keys. Pneumatically controlled actions have been used, and chimes can also be played from a small piano-type keyboard which operates the clappers electrically through the solenoids. These systems allow the player little or no scope for expression and interpretation. However, modern carillons achieve the essentials by such devices as springs, counterbalances and ball-bearings incorporated in the action, so that physical effort is reduced but the vital link between man and machine maintained.

On a true carillon of twenty-four bells or more the carilloneur makes use not only of his hands but also of his feet. The foot-pedals are connected to the heavier bells, enabling a bass-line to be played below the melody of the lighter bells.

In Belgium and the Netherlands bells in carillons are often mounted in the openings of a tower instead of together in a frame inside it, a device which while architecturally attractive is not satisfying musically as the listener hears to advantage only the bells nearest him. The action is also made more difficult and requires great physical strength—even for a conventionally constructed carillon the player's hand has to be protected with a leather covering to avoid injury to the fingers. Small wonder that a Dutch writer, Fischer, observed in 1738 that 'for carillon playing a man requires nothing more than a thorough knowledge of music, good hands and feet, and no gout'! In Britain, and in other countries where expert carilloneurs are hard to find, the electrically operated keyboard is used or an automatic device which plays selected tunes. This is often a roll of 'music' rather like that used for the old player-pianos, or in the form of a rotating drum with teeth, and can be set in advance to play a tune or hymn at a pre-determined time. Generally there is a combination of automation and keyboard, so that true carillon-playing may be indulged in by a carilloneur and at other times the tunes are produced automatically. There are about a dozen carillons with claviers in Britain, one of the best known to Londoners being the instrument at the premises of Atkinson's, the perfume-makers in Bond Street, installed in 1926. At the Odeon Cinema, Marble Arch, there was formerly a thirty-two-bell carillon mounted just off-stage and played from the organ console, which unfortunately has now been dismantled and shipped to Belgium. Birmingham has a well-known carillon at the Church of Our Lady of the Rosary, Saltley, on which recitals are given during the winter months on Thursdays and Sundays.

## Chimes in Britain

There are many chimes in Britain played purely automatically, and these include the famous bells of London's Royal Exchange, rung electrically since 1921, and the chimes at the modern civic centre at Newcastle upon Tyne, with its heavy set of twenty-five bells with a 71cwt tenor.

It is, of course, possible to install or adapt conventional church bells to be chimed automatically, and this has been done in several churches where the services of ringers are not available, or not required.

A famous set of bells in an even more famous church which is now sounded this way is at All Hallows, on Tower Hill in London. Here there has been a church for nearly thirteen cen-

turies—since the first, humble building was dedicated by St
Ethelburga, Abbess of Barking, in 675. It successfully survived
the Reformation, but suffered greatly from the results of an
explosion on Tower Hill in 1649, possibly of political origin
as in another part of London Charles I was being tried that day.
The explosion wrecked the tower and its five bells, but these
were recast into a ring of six and installed in a new tower ten
years later. There they remained until 1813, when they were
again recast, and this time augmented to eight by the Whitechapel foundry.

During World War I the church became associated with
Toc H, the servicemen's association, and in 1922 its founder
the Rev 'Tubby' Clayton, became vicar. In 1940 the church
was gutted by incendiary bombs. Fortunately the outer shell of
the nave and tower remained, and after World War II magnificent work of reconstruction was undertaken. But the tower,
still standing, and though strengthened, was still considered
too dangerous for the swing of heavy bells and it was decided
to install a ring hung 'dead' for chiming. The cost was met by
a large legacy from John McConnell of Montreal, and in 1948
a fine chime of eighteen bells, cast by Taylor's of Loughborough, was installed in the church. Though the bells may be
played automatically by an electro-pneumatic device, All
Hallows is fortunate in having the services of an expert carilloneur who gives regular recitals.

On the opposite side of Aldgate another chime exists on the
premises of the Houndsditch Warehouse Company Ltd. Here
there is a ring of ten hung for chiming, with a 4½cwt tenor;
but in this area of wholesale transactions and down-to-earth-
dealings the ringing of the till is more common than the sound
of bells, and the chimes have been silent these many years.

The two biggest carillons in Britain are found at Bournville
Schools, Birmingham, and at the Church of St Nicholas,
Aberdeen, each with forty-eight bells. Aberdeen has the heavier
bells, and the tenor, at 89cwt, is the heaviest carillon bell in the
country.

In several parish churches devices have been installed which chime the bells automatically, usually for the performance of short lengths of methods as tunes are rarely possible on less than eight bells. At the church of St Cyr, at Stinchcombe, Gloucestershire, an electronic machine was installed in the 1960s during a period when the village had no ringers and there was talk of disposing of the bells. The legal wrangle that ensued created such publicity that now the village has a full complement of ringers and the machine is therefore rarely required! The instrument, contained in a small wall-case at the foot of the tower, is worked from two punched tapes which allow electrical contact to be made with the clappers of the bells as the tape moves along. The tapes are punched in such a way as to correspond with the ringing of the bells in a method, and, in fact look rather like a series of changes 'pricked out' on paper as described earlier.

Automatic methods of ringing are, for obvious reasons, not looked on kindly by most bellringers, though the reason for their existence is nearly always that there is a lack of ringers in the parish concerned. Worst of all, according to most ringers, is the playing of a tape-recorded peal from a tower which has no bells, or perhaps only one or two. The general public may consider this is preferable to the jangling of real bells by inexperienced ringers, for the tape used in such instances is likely to be a recording of a good band ringing in a tower such as St Margaret's, Westminster, or Southwark Cathedral—and few can object to ringing of that standard.

## Carillons and Chimes Overseas

Overseas, where conventional full-circle ringing is unknown, automatic ringing is taken much more seriously and chimes and carillons are common. While the tradition of the carillon is particularly strong in Holland and Belgium it has latterly become popular in America and Australia, which have about

200 carillons between them, including some of the largest and finest in the world.

The largest carillon in existence is the seventy-four bell instrument of the Laura Rockefeller Memorial carillon at Riverside Drive Church, New York, installed by Gillet & Johnston of Croydon in 1930. This magnificent carillon was presented by John D. Rockefeller in memory of his mother. Two years later the University of Chicago expressed a desire to have a carillon, and Rockefeller, having been educated there, offered to give them one on the understanding that it would not be as large as the New York carillon. The offer was accepted, and though Chicago has seventy-two bells (the same number that Riverside Church had originally) the tenor bell is lighter. Gillett & Johnson still service these great carillons and late in 1972 a major overhaul and rehanging of the New York bells was begun by this firm. Other famous American carillons are at Niagara Falls (the Peace Tower) and at the Singing Tower, Lake Wales, Florida. Most recently installed (1962) is the Grand Carillon of the National Episcopal Church at Washington DC, made by Taylor's of Loughborough.

In 1970 Taylor's foundry installed the fifty-three-bell Canberra Carillon at Aspen Island, CT, Australia, a gift from the British government to mark the city's golden jubilee. The carillon is housed in a tower in the central basin of Lake Burley Griffin, near the site of the new Houses of Parliament and the tower itself, also the gift of the British government, was designed by an Australian firm of architects in open competition. In addition to the four-and-a-half octave clavier there is an automatic playing mechanism designed and manufactured by the firm of Korfhage of Osnabrück, Germany, which will provide music for a total of twenty hours and includes such familiar tunes as 'Waltzing Matilda', 'The Minstrel Boy', 'Men of Harlech', 'Scotland the Brave' and 'Greensleeves'—a truly international selection.

Carillon music, played from the clavier, is capable of great versatility and on a large instrument may range from simple folk tunes to classical music in three parts. It is usually undertaken by a specialist musician who has probably passed through the Carillon School at Mechelen (Malines) in Belgium, founded by Jef Denyn, one of the world's greatest carilloneurs.

In Europe, as already said, the sound of the carillon is taken rather more seriously than in England, and is appreciated much more. Admittedly, the authorities at Newcastle upon Tyne have made available taped recordings of their civic centre carillon playing 'Northumberland' and other airs, which have sold well. But it will be a long time before the scene is re-enacted in Britain, so common abroad, when the entire traffic of a town comes to a halt at the sound of the carillon, and everyone just stands and listens.

(*right*) The tenor bell of St Botolph's parish church, Boston, Lincs (the famous 'Boston Stump') as recast by Taylor's in 1932. The cost was shared by the people of Boston, Lincs and those of Boston, Mass, USA

THIS PEAL OF TEN BELLS WAS CAST
FROM THE FORMER PEAL OF EIGHT AT
THE JOINT EXPENSE OF THE PEOPLE OF
BOSTON, MASS, U.S.A. AND BOSTON, LINCS

ALLAN FORBES, CHAIRMAN, BOSTON, MASS
JAMES TAIT, CHAIRMAN, BOSTON, LINCS
A. M. COOK, M.A., VICAR
1932

THE CORONATION BELL OF HIS MAJESTY
KING GEORGE VI
RECAST BY
FREEMASONS OF LEICESTERSHIRE AND RUTLAND
12 MAY 1937

F. E. McNUTT                C. T. OLIVER
PROVOST            PROVINCIAL G.M.

GOD SAVE THE KING.

(*left*) The recast tenor bell of Leicester Cathedral presented by the Freemasons of Leicestershire and Rutland for the coronation of Edward VIII in 1937. Owing to the abdication of the King in December 1936, Edward's name was blocked-out and that of King George VI substituted, as indicated by the lighter letters

(*left*) The massive frame and bells of the new carillon for Canberra, ACT at the foundry prior to shipment to Australia (*below*) Mr Paul Taylor, of the Loughborough Bell Foundry, testing the clavier of the Canberra carillon

Page 119 (above) P. van den Broek, a famous Dutch carilloneur, at the clavier of the carillon at Mechelen; (below) the bells at Washington Cathedral, USA. Note that they are hung radially, all swinging towards the centre, to eliminate stress

*Page 120* The surprisingly English-looking new cathedral at Washington DC (USA)

# HANDBELL-RINGING

The College Youths' excursion overseas to Calais in 1732 to ring handbells was an important event in ringing circles. It signalled the first recorded occasion on which changes were rung on handbells to the same rules and specifications that applied to tower bells.

Handbells, as we have seen, were one of the earliest forms of bells and were in existence long before tower bells. The Bayeux tapestry shows a boy on each side of the coffin carrying a handbell, and their use by night-watchmen, town criers and the like was common practice throughout Europe. Sets of bells, tuned to scale, were also popular: the Worms Bible of 1148 illustrates a set of eight bells, suspended from a beam, on which a tune is being 'tapped' with a small hammer. The illustration has additional interest in that the note of each bell of the octave is indicated above it.

With the coming of change-ringing on church bells it was quickly realised that handbells represented an easy and practical way of learning the intricacies of peals without having to try them out first on tower bells. The method could be memorised and practised on handbells, though of course the physical problems of ringing the method on tower bells could only be overcome in the belfry itself. Still, it was a useful exercise, and it was not long before the ringing of methods on handbells came to be regarded as an art in itself.

Handbells light enough to be rung 'in hand'—as distinct from those that were hung and 'tapped'—and tuned to scale were probably first produced in England at the Wiltshire foundry of the Corr family about 1700. Today's handbells have not changed much from the first design. The alloy used is 80 per cent copper and 20 per cent tin; the handle is usually a double leather strap, and the clapper is tipped with leather or wood pegs so that metal never comes in contact with metal during ringing. This preserves the mellow note that is so characteristic of handbells and at the same time allows the harmonic over-tones to be heard. As with tower bells, handbells increase in size according to the depth of their note. The great difference, how-ever, is that whilst tower bells are limited to a maximum of twelve for all practical purposes, handbells are not restricted to any specific number in a set. In practice they are made to cover a total of five chromatic octaves, sixty-one bells in all, and vary in weight from 4oz to 10lb. It is rare to find a com-plete set of handbells of such a wide range in actual use, and the normal range covers two octaves, with the lightest bell being about 8oz and the heaviest 2lb. Each ringer rings two handbells, and in the early days of handbell-ringing the tunes were 'pricked out' on paper much in the same way as methods were set out for tower ringers. But there the resemblance ends, for the strict rules of method-ringing did not apply and the bells changed places solely in accordance with the notes of the tune. Handbells, being light and mobile, also lent themselves admirably to experiment and could be rung almost anywhere. There is an account of 1758 in which the band at Shifnal in Nottinghamshire rang a 1,008 Bob Major in the house of one of the ringers, John Nock. The host rang 1 and 2 in the parlour, John Debney rang 3 and 4 in the brewhouse, Samuel Lawrence 5 and 6 standing in the bedroom and Thomas Clemson weighed in on 7 and 8 in the cellar! Each ringer was out of sight of the others, and the accomplishment, possibly done for a wager, indicates a high standard of handbell-ringing. Freak attempts such as this have always been popular with handbell-ringers, and at a much later date (1923) a band of Cumberland Youths embarked on a handbell peal of 5,056 Bob Major in a train leaving Paddington at 6pm, completing the peal and coming into rounds two hours and twenty-two minutes later as the train drew into the station at Stroud, Gloucestershire! The peal had the distinction (for what it was worth) of having been rung in six counties.

Peal attempts on handbells feature regularly in the pages of the *Ringing World* and are accepted by the Central Council. But in 1920 a certain Arthur Morris, a ringer of Harwich, Essex, really 'put the cat among the pigeons' by tapping peals on handbells in his home instead of ringing them by hand in what had come to be the orthodox manner. These peals were submitted to the Central Council, but this august body refused to recognise their validity due to the method by which they had been achieved. The local Essex Association took their cue from the Central Council and so precipitated the most heated and bitter argument ever experienced in ringing circles. In the *Ringing World* correspondence became almost hysterical in its intensity and inevitably descended to personalities to the extent that by the end of 1921 the editor was forced to terminate it on the grounds that 'the consequences of infringement of the law of libel may well fall upon the publisher as well as the writer'. Arthur Morris resigned from the Essex Association, though he continued submitting 'tapped' peals, and died in 1923 bitter and disillusioned. It is a sad story, and indicates the intensity of feeling and emotion that can be aroused amongst those who live only for their hobby.

The ringing of handbells as a band, for the playing of tunes and hymns, is more likely to prove a relaxation than to engender the high feelings experienced by Mr Morris and the 'scientific' ringers of his day. The ringing of recognisable tunes on hand-bells became a popular pastime in towns and villages during the second half of the eighteenth century. By the time of Queen

Victoria's accession competitions were being organised between handbell bands, and handbell concerts were being given to enthusiastic audiences. In the North of England, in particular, handbells were extremely popular and handbell concerts and competitions were held regularly from 1826 in the famous Belle Vue Gardens in Manchester—for a hundred years the entertainment and cultural centre of the area. So great was the enthusiasm that handbell-ringing at Belle Vue became the northern equivalent of London's Crystal Palace, the great centre for brass band concerts and choir festivals in the south. Among some the most proficient bands at Manchester were the Yorkshire ringers, and those from Cheshire and Lancashire. So famous did the Lancashire ringers become that in 1845 the great American showman, P. T. Barnum, engaged them for a tour of the United States. Not content with demonstrating their prowess on handbells Barnum insisted on dressing the members of the band in Swiss peasant costume and billed them as 'the famous Swiss Bell Ringers'! Since that time handbells have been related in the popular imagination with Switzerland, a misconception that dies hard. Less publicised but equally successful in America at about the same time were four of the Peake family of Yorkshire who gave concerts and demonstrations. They were the first handbell-ringers to be seen in America, and the Lancashire Ringers, many of whom were tower bellringers as well, demonstrated the more serious side of the art by being the first handbell team to ring a standard peal of 5,040 changes in the United States.

Round the turn of the century various methods of ringing handbells were in use which did not involve picking up the bells 'in hand' and ringing them in the orthodox manner. One such method was 'lapping' and another was 'rolling'. In 'lapping' the ringers sat in a row, each man with two bells in his lap, and when ringing would lift his bell enough for it to sound, after which he placed it in the lap of another ringer according to whatever method was being followed. In this way each man rang two bells, one after the other, from one end of

the row to the other, but it was the bells themselves that
changed places and produced the requisite changes in the right
order. 'Rolling' again involved the physical movement of the
bells changing places, but this time it was done with the bells
arranged in a row on a long table, 'rolling' one over the other at
each change. But mostly, for solo performance, the method of
choice was 'tapping', and many famous exponents of the art
emerged during late-Victorian and Edwardian times. The bells
were hung suspended on a frame, and the player would 'tap'
each in turn with a light hammer at an astonishing speed producing long and complicated methods to the delight of his
audience. When one remembers that these peals were rung
without any visual assistance from watching other ringers, as
in tower bell-ringing, and with no guide or captain to correct
a mistake, tapping a peal of 5,000 and more changes this way
was an astonishing feat of mental concentration.

After World War I handbell ringing suffered a decline in
Britain, apart from the controversial exploits of Arthur
Morris. A few village schools maintained a band for the purpose
of ringing carols at Christmastime or for special occasions, but
on the whole handbells became considered an out-of-date
method of making music and by 1926 the last handbell
festival had been held at Belle Vue.

As has happened so often, America gave a new lease of life
to a dying English tradition. In 1923 Mrs Margaret Shurcliff
of Boston came to Britain to ring church bells with the College
Youths and was presented by them with a magnificent set of
handbells to take back with her. Once home, Mrs Shurcliff
(who incidentally, was one of the first women to ring a peal on
tower bells in England) formed the Beacon Hill Ringers of
Boston, an organisation still very much alive today.

For some years handbell-ringing in America was confined to
the New England states, but during the last twenty years it
has spread enormously and has been taken up enthusiastically
all over the country. Today one of the most famous teams is
the Potomac English Handbell Ringers led by Mrs Nancy

Tufts, author of an excellent book on handbell-ringing. This team travels over a wide area giving displays; they are dressed not as Swiss peasants but in colourful Tudor costume. Another famous band is the Wesley Bell Choir of the Central Church, Springfield, Ohio. In 1954 the American Guild of English Handbell Ringers was formed and it is estimated that today there are over 500 handbell teams in the United States, with probably 5,000 active ringers.

In England, after being in the doldrums between the wars, handbell-ringing experienced a revival from the early sixties onwards. Handbell teams have been formed in many villages by the wives of the bellringers of the church, and the band thus assembled at Braunton in Devon, consisting entirely of ladies, has been instrumental in raising much money for the church and other charitable causes. Handbell-ringing is also being used by occupational therapists and others as a means of rehabilitation and is a popular activity in many centres for disabled people and also for the blind.

Probably the most famous handbell-ringers in Britain at the present time are those at Launton in Oxfordshire, led by that doyen of ringers Mr Frederick Sharpe, a member of the Central Council and a most learned and prolific writer on bells and their history. Launton ringers have appeared frequently on radio and television programmes, and in December 1971 they appeared in a radio programme arranged by the Central Office of Information which was broadcast in every country in the world excepting China and the USSR.

Handbells have not been used extensively by composers, and certainly not in multiple form. A notable exception is Benjamin Britten's *Noyes Fludde*, the opera based on the sixteenth-century Chester mystery play. The score includes a fairly complicated passage for handbells and it has come as a surprise to more than one conductor to hear how expertly the bells are handled, often by very young ringers.

One of the largest sets of handbells in existence is owned by the village of Ecclesfield, near Sheffield: no less than 163 have

been collected there since 1905. Many of these bells were part
of the original set which performed so valiantly at the great
Belle Vue festivals early in the century. For some reason this
village seems to have developed a strong tradition for handbell-
ringing, and the Ecclesfield Secondary School (now incor-
porating the Grammar School) has a splendid five-octave set of
sixty-one bells ranging from the tintinnabulous 4in treble to
the sonorous 10lb tenor. In 1971 the school, under the enthusiastic leadership of Michael King, one of the staff, raised
£350 for the recasting of the entire set of bells by the Whitechapel foundry, and this is one of the finest sets of handbells to
be found anywhere in Britain today. Another large set of
handbells is at Thurlestone, near Penistone, also in Yorkshire,
where a healthy tradition continues.

Curiously enough, though handbell-ringing is experiencing
such a revival in England, there is as yet no central organisation
for ringers as there is for church bellringers. Yet even in 1965
enthusiasm was sufficient to encourage the first handbell-
ringers' rally, which has since become an annual event. Ringers
are certainly not confined to the north of England, and teams
are welcomed from places as far apart as Folkestone, Alton
(Hampshire) and Great Glen (Scotland). At the 1970 rally
over 1,000 competitors attended, a high proportion of them
children. It seems almost as if the great days of Belle Vue are
coming back. Indeed, at the East of England handbell rally held
at Rougham, Suffolk, in 1972, the MC for the day, Leonard
Last, started the proceedings by describing to an enthralled
audience of young ringers his experiences at the last handbell
rally he had attended—at Belle Vue, Manchester, fifty years
before!

CHAPTER 12

# RINGING OVERSEAS

## *India and Pakistan*

The empire-builders of the nineteenth century, in their frantic
efforts to avoid the setting sun, had little time for such refinements as bellringing. Churches were built, of course, but
lamentably few were provided with a ringable set of bells. In
India, for example, only at Poona, at the church of the Holy
Name at Panch Howd, is there a ring of eight, but these bells
are only suitable for chiming. In Pakistan, Lahore Cathedral is
more fortunate in having a ring of six bells, including an 18cwt
tenor, which is in good condition. Singapore's St Andrew's
Cathedral was presented with an eight-bell ring in 1889 in
memory of a Captain Fraser of the East India Company's Service, and to mark the seventieth anniversary of the founding of
the settlement. The ring is fairly heavy, with a 28cwt tenor,
and not long after the dedication it was discovered that the
foundations and masonry of the tower could not withstand the
strain of full-circle ringing. A chiming apparatus was specially
made by Taylor's of Loughborough, who cast the bells, and it
is by this means that they are rung today.

## Australia and New Zealand

It is in Australia and New Zealand, where the British way of
life was brought by early settlers and adapted to the very
different conditions that existed, that bellringing flourishes
most outside England. In Australia twenty-seven towers, all
ringable except two, provide a basis for the Australian and
New Zealand Association of Bellringers, and these are augmented by four New Zealand rings out of the six bell-towers
existing in that country.

Most of the Australian rings are situated in New South
Wales and Victoria, and though distances seem great by English
standards, regular visits are made by ringers and there is an
annual ringing festival which all of them may attend. Perth,
in Western Australia, is the most isolated, being 1,500 miles
from its nearest ringing neighbour in Adelaide. The ringers
of the nine-bell tower at Maryborough, Queensland, must
travel over 500 miles to visit their nearest tower at Maitland,
New South Wales. From there it is only another 100 miles to
Sydney, where the greatest concentration of ringing towers in
Australia is found. Sydney and its suburbs can provide ten
rings, all in good condition and in regular use. These include
a fine ring of ten at St Andrew's Cathedral, and a ring of eight
at the Roman Catholic Basilica of St Mary—the bells of this
latter church were the ones that rang out to welcome Pope Paul
on his visit to Australia in November 1970 and created so
much interest in the Australian Press. One ringer was reported
to have come by air 800 miles from Adelaide specially to take
part in the peal, returning home the same evening!

In Melbourne the triple-spired Cathedral of St Paul's domi-
nates the city, and its massive main tower includes the only
ring of twelve outside the British Isles. The bells were cast by
the Whitechapel Bell Foundry in 1889 and the cathedral stands
on the very spot where, in 1836, a Scottish doctor conducted—
from a tent—the first 'official' church service in Melbourne.

H

In 1934 great impetus was given to Australian ringing by the first organised visit of a band from England and for the first time a complete peal was rung on Melbourne cathedral's twelve bells. The band consisted of six English and six Australian ringers, and was led by J. S. Goldsmith, at that time editor and owner of the *Ringing World*, who dubbed it 'The Great Adventure'.

Just over thirty years later, in 1965, the second organised bellringing visit to Australia took place, which this time included New Zealand. Today, ringers from England are found in increasing numbers in Australian towers while on business or on holiday.

But not all Australian bells are in church towers. One of the most important ringing towers is that of the city hall in Ballarat. Its bells have a curious origin. In 1868 Prince Alfred, one of Queen Victoria's four sons, narrowly escaped assassination in Sydney. He had previously visited Ballarat, and the townsfolk, with commendable patriotism, determined to express their thanks for his delivery by purchasing 'a peal of eight bells to be called the Alfred Memorial Bells, to be erected in Ballarat with a suitable inscription recording the attack'. Rather optimistically the bells were ordered from Whitechapel before sufficient funds were raised, and when delivery took place the following year no tower had yet been built to house them and no funds were available to pay for them! Fortunately it was decided to build a new town hall, and the onus of paying for the bells and finding them a suitable home was taken over by the city council, which incorporated them in the new building. At 6 o'clock on Christmas morning 1871, the bells of Ballarat rang out for the first time. They are still rung by an enthusiastic local band, who were joined by the equally enthusiastic ringers from Bendigo to celebrate the centenary of the bells in 1971. It is encouraging to note that the number of bells in Australia is increasing, and in November 1970 a completely new ring of eight was dedicated at St Cuthbert's church at Prospect near Adelaide. It is hoped that some of the unringable bells that exist, like those in Melbourne's 'old' cathedral, may be salvaged. In the meantime plans are afoot to have the ring of eight at the town hall in Adelaide recast and rehung. As usual, finance is the problem; the cost of carrying out this work is enormous quite apart from transportation to Britain and back. In Tasmania there are two good rings at Hobart.

In 1972 the ringers of ANZAB decided to make their annual ringing festival a tour of New Zealand. Admittedly, there are only four towers where bells can properly be rung, but with the addition of handbell-ringing the tour was justified and was a distinct success. Two of New Zealand's four rings are at Christchurch, the more picturesque tower being that of St Paul's, Papanui, a trim weather-boarded church opened in 1877. (The Maoris gave the name Papanui to the settlement from the extensive native timber industry in the surrounding swampland, *papa* meaning flat and *nui* board.) The bells were installed in 1880 but once again lack of technical knowledge resulted in a dangerous swaying of the timber tower and the eventual banning of the bells. Later an iron gantry embedded in concrete was provided, from which the bells were hung, and the tower is today perfectly safe. Though Papanui bells have been rung on and off for nearly ninety years it was only in 1965 that a regular ringing association was formed. Most ringing had been carried out by the ringers of Christchurch Cathedral, whose ring of ten with a 32 cwt tenor is only a year younger than Papanui's bells.

Over 500 miles away, on North Island, are New Zealand's two other ringable towers, at Hamilton and Auckland. South of Hamilton, at Cambridge, six steel bells are hung in the timber tower of the church, but they are mounted in such a way as to make a full swing impossible. The tower is also officially listed as 'unsafe'.

## The United States

Making 'improvements' to a tower in such a way that the
bells are made unringable not only happens in New Zealand.
It is also considered a form of progress in some American
churches and has reduced the usable rings in the United States
from twelve to eight. The situation is particularly unfortunate
in Boston, where three rings of eight bells exist but cannot be
used. Most historic is the ring in Boston's Old North Church
(Emmanuel)—the first set of bells to be shipped to the colonies
before the War of Independence. Ironically it is the very importance of this church in the history of the United States that
now prevents the ringing of the bells. The pipes of the modern
sprinkler system that has been installed run through the spokes of
the wheels on which the bells are mounted! It is doubly ironical
that Paul Revere, the hero of the War of Independence and a
bell-founder, was actually a ringer in this very church. His
ringing of these bells can almost be said to have changed the
course of history.

There is another ring of eight at the Church of the Advent,
Boston, but their use is restricted to chiming only owing to
insecure hanging. They came from the Whitechapel foundry
and there is a possibility that in the foreseeable future they
may be rehung and used again. Boston's third ring of eight is
housed in an enormous tower at the centre of the vast Perkins
Institute for the Blind. With a 22cwt tenor they form a
slightly heavier ring than the other two, and are said to be in
good condition. Unfortunately the director of the institute has
so far refused permission for these bells to be rung for fear of
annoying local residents.

Though Boston may represent the refinement in frustration
for American ringers there are compensations in other rings
along the Atlantic seaboard. One of the most pleasing is the
light ring of eight installed recently in the tower of Smith's
Ladies College at Northampton, Massachusetts. They form

part of the university's superbly equipped complex known as the Centre for Performing Arts and are accorded the status due to them. Indeed, there are two practice nights here each week, something that would precipitate an instant protest if it happened in any English tower. Also in Massachusetts is a ring of ten housed in the very tall and unbuttressed tower of the Memorial Hall at Hingham, where the long draught together with the distinctly felt movement of the tower makes it a difficult ring on which to learn. Nevertheless ringing is regular for Sunday morning service and a keen band is maintained.

The school chapel at Groton, Massachusetts, also has a ring of ten from Whitechapel which is reported to be an excellent ring but suffering from neglect. This is certainly not the situation at the school chapel at Kent, Connecticut, where the ring of ten is housed picturesquely on a wooded hillside overlooking the school buildings. The 25cwt tenor represents a challenge for young boys wishing to learn, but enthusiasm is such that the bells are rung each evening during term. Admittedly this is a situation in which local 'residents' are hardly in a position to complain!

Christ Church, Philadelphia, has a ring of eight bells whose sound has not been heard for over thirty years. Just before the war a new organ was installed, and to accommodate the pipes the floor of the ringing chamber was removed. Further south the bells of St Michael's in Charleston, South Carolina, have also been made unringable, this time by the installation of a chiming apparatus which does, at least, allow their sound to be heard. Nearly 1,000 miles away, at Houston, Texas, the bells are being heard for the first time, for a ring of eight was installed in 1971 in the tower of St Thomas's Episcopal Church. In the absence of any experienced ringers it is a long, hard haul for learners in this tower to teach themselves the art of ringing and its says much for their enthusiasm that some were able to join a party of American ringers visiting England in 1972.

Another 'lone' tower on the vast expanse of the North American continent is that at the University of Chicago, 500 miles from its nearest neighbour at Washington, DC. In the university's Mitchell Tower a 22cwt tenor heads the ring of ten installed in 1910, which, through lack of use, became very difficult to ring. Once again enthusiasm is prevailing over lack of experience, and a competent band of learners is forming.

America's most famous bells are those at Washington's Episcopal Cathedral, installed in 1963 and first rung by a band from England on 9 May 1964. They are a heavy ring of ten, with a 32cwt tenor, and were cast by the Whitechapel foundry. A second set of bells, hung for use as a carillon, was cast by Taylor's of Loughborough and so provides examples of bells from the only two English bell-foundries still in existence. It is no surprise that in a modern building such as this, ringing can be done in ideal conditions—there is even a lift giving access to the ringing chamber. The church attracts many enthusiasts, particularly from Britain.

# Canada

Ringing-towers in Canada are fewer and further between than in the United States. The six rings which are usable extend from the Gulf of St Lawrence to Vancouver Island and include, surprisingly, a mid-West ring at Calgary. In the beautiful city of Quebec two rings of eight exist, one in the Anglican Cathedral of the Holy Trinity and the other in the church of St Matthew. Regular ringing takes place only at the cathedral, though occasional visits are made by the cathedral ringers to St Matthew's. In Montreal the situation is different. The only two rings of bells, in the Roman Catholic churches of Notre Dame and St Patrick, are both unsuitable for full-circle ringing. Notre Dame, with a tenor weighing 52cwt, boasts the second heaviest ring of ten in the world and in addition has a separate bourdon bell for tolling, weighing 11½ tons.

For the next nearest usable ring of bells in Canada one must travel nearly 2,000 miles west to Calgary, where Christ Church,

Elbow Park, has a modern and light ring of eight. Ringing here is regular, though difficulties arise during the winter months when extremes of cold can cause the grease to solidify in the bearings.

British Columbia is fortunate in having three fine rings of bells. The Roman Catholic cathedral in Vancouver has an interesting ring of eight rehung in 1906 and recast from the original ring of five installed in 1900. At Victoria, Christ Church Cathedral has a near-perfect ring of eight with a 29cwt tenor and a band keen enough to provide regular Sunday ringing and a week-night practice. The third ring is at Mission City, some fifty miles from Vancouver, where a modern ring of ten bells hangs in the fluted concrete tower of the Roman Catholic Westminster Abbey. In this Benedictine community there is no problem in finding ringers, for the bells are rung regularly by the monks themselves. It is hoped that the school attached will eventually provide more ringers.

## *Africa*

While the Australian and North American continents may between them have the greatest number of bells outside Britain, Africa maintains the highest percentage of ringable bells from those available. For though there are only eight rings of bells in the whole continent, each one is usable. Most famous is the ring of ten at the Cathedral of St Mary and All Saints, Salisbury, Southern Rhodesia. The first Anglican church service was held in Salisbury in 1890, yet it took seventy years for a permanent church to be completed and the bells installed. The present cathedral was begun in 1913, only to be halted by World War I and the economic problems that followed. Not until 1938 did building recommence—this time to be stopped by World War II. Building began again in 1954, inspired by the gift of a ring of ten bells from 'an English friend' whose identity is unknown to this day. The gift, generous as it was,

created an added difficulty: even more funds were now required
to build a suitable bell-tower. This problem was eventually
overcome and the bells were installed in 1961, the cathedral
itself being completed in 1964.

At the southern end of the continent Cape Town has two
rings, one of eight at the industrial centre of Woodstock, the
other of ten in St George's Cathedral. Grahamstown, Cape
Province, has a ringable eight in the timber tower of its small
cathedral.

Durban, Natal, has a ring of ten at St Mary, Greyville, and
another of eight at St Paul's, with regular ringing at both.
Less regular is the ringing at the remote Kenyan church of St
Thomas at Kilifi, where the very light ring of six (tenor 2cwt)
is hung exposed to the elements, and at Que-Que, Rhodesia,
which has a ring of only four bells. The regular ringing at
Durban may be due in part to the enthusiasm of emigrant
ringers from England of a generation ago, for immediately
after the war, in 1946, this advertisement appeared in *Ringing
World*: 'Half-a-dozen or more ringers wanted to settle in
Durban. Assistance given to find employment.' It would be
pleasant to think that the ringers of Durban are today the
sons and daughters of those post-war pilgrim ringers.

## *Europe*

For reasons which have already been explained there are virtually no bells hung for full-circle ringing in Europe. Yet there
is one odd exception. In the tiny parish church of Rivoli
Veronese, in northern Italy, hangs a ring of five bells, each
mounted on a wheel and capable of being rung in peal, though
they have no stay or slider. They are used frequently by the
villagers, mainly for their own enjoyment, and with an enthusiasm that is no less real for never having heard of Stedman
or Double Norwich Court Bob. The origin of these bells
remains a mystery, and the implications intriguing. For if the

villagers think about it long enough they, too, will become fascinated by the permutations possible on five and more bells. It would be interesting, if, 300 years after Stedman, an Italian school of method-ringing were to evolve.

CHAPTER 13

# THAT'S ALL!

Public consciousness of bellringing and all it involves is gradually awakening—but it is a long and painful process. Even when consciousness is awakened it does not necessarily mean that approval goes with it, and though romantically minded writers and poets have often eulogised the sound of bells their enthusiasm is not shared by all literary men.

Thomas Hardy, for example, left the reader in little doubt as to his views on bells when he suggested the following set of inscriptions for a recast ring of eight in a Dorset village:

1 Thomas Tremble new-made me
Eighteen hundred and fifty-three:
Why he did I fail to see.

2 I was well-toned by William Brine
Seventeen-hundred and twenty-nine;
Now re-cast I weakly whine!

3 Fifteen-hundred used to be my date,
But since they melted me—
Eighteen fifty-three.

4 Henry Hopkins got me made
And I summon folk as bade;
Not to much purpose, I'm afraid!

5   I, likewise, for I bang and bid
    In commoner metal than I did,
    Some of me being stole and hid.

6   I, too, since in a mould they flung me,
    Drained my silver and re-hung me,
    So that in tin-like tones I tongue me.

7   In eighteen-hundred, so 'tis said,
    They cut my cannons off my head,
    And made me look scalped, scraped and dead.

8   I'm the peal's tenor still, but rue it;
    Once it took two to swing me through it:
    Now I'm re-hung one dolt can do it!

An artistic temperament does not always go hand-in-hand
with a love of bells, and in Buckinghamshire a certain well-
known painter, disturbed by the ringing of bells on practice
night, threatened to install an amplifier on the flat roof of his
house and play Beethoven in retaliation!

The BBC's new awareness of ringing and ringing matters is
encouraging, and the fuller details of peals and towers now
given when introducing church services may well awaken
interest and a desire to know more. A public-relations exercise
of a very different kind may be seen in Leicester in the Bell
Bar of the grandiose Post House in Narborough Road. The
Post House continues the tradition of the now vanished Bell
Hotel in the city and includes several items from it. It claims
(and probably justly) to have the only 'campanologists' carpet'
in any bar in Britain. Designed by Allan Ballantyne, it features
a series of rectangles of different sizes and patterns based on
the change-ringing method of Double Bob Minor. Bellringing
is featured again in the curtains, where the motif is a series of
zigzag lines taken from the 'pricked-out' diagram of bells performing a Plain Hunt. An additional touch of colour in this
unusual room comes from the bright red and green sallies on
their ropes used for decorating the walls. It is no surprise to
discover that the architect of the Post House, John Sanson, is

himself a ringer. Leicester, of course, has one of the longest traditions of bell-founding in Britain and, through the years the county has supplied more bells than anywhere else in England outside London. This may well be the reason for this imaginative form of decoration, for though 'The Bell' is a very common name for inns and hostelries it is rare to find any other reference to ringing on the premises apart from the bells depicted on the sign. Even on inn-signs the bell is often a caricature of what a real bell should be, and only a few dedicated inn-sign artists can be trusted to portray them accurately. An interest in ringing may be aroused by a visit to the Science Museum in London, where a curious mechanical instrument called the 'Campanutophone' is on display. This ingenious machine can be made to ring almost any known method automatically and to demonstrate the work of selected bells, isolating them from the main stream. It was made by a Mr Carter early this century and was first demonstrated publicly at a dinner of the Ancient Society of College Youths in 1921.

In theory, at least, it is the Central Council of Church Bell Ringers which disseminates information on the Exercise to the non-converted, and the appropriate committee of this body supplies the Press with information when requested, and makes representations to the BBC for more accuracy and information regarding the broadcasting of bells and peals. The Central Council was formed in 1891 at the instigation of that great ringer and expert on church architecture, Sir Arthur Heywood, who was the first president for twenty-five years until his death in 1916. Other ringers in the past have also shed light on the mysteries of ringing by writing books, one of the best-known series being that of Jasper Snowdon, though few deal with the historical background but are concerned primarily with the improvement of technique and the discussion of the more abstruse problems of composition and conducting. One splendid exception is the *History and Art of Change-Ringing* by the late Ernest Morris of Leicester, which deals not only with the intricacies and technicalities of ringing but is a mine of information on famous Victorian ringers and ringing traditions. Ernest Morris, incidentally, was not only an expert on ringing history but a specialist on many subjects including fonts, door-knockers and horse-brasses, all of which are faithfully depicted in the memorial window to him in St Margaret's, Leicester, where he died in 1962. Some churches have a band of young ringers whose enthusiasm has been aroused by a talk or demonstration at school, or by attending a handbell demonstration. Some may not be interested, some may begin but fall by the wayside, and a few may continue as infant prodigies, appearing in the *Ringing World* after ringing their first three-hour peal at the age of twelve. Infant prodigies tend not to remain prodigies for long, but an aptitude for ringing in a very young person can create problems when enthusiasm comes into conflict with academic objectives. Ringing is a hobby which can be fatally enticing to the exclusion of almost everything else.

But the greatest help to the development of the ringer is the company of a good band with a wise and patient tower-captain. In addition there must be co-operation, even if not exactly enthusiasm, on the part of the incumbent, for, after all, it is *his* tower and *his* bells and it is he, and not the Parochial Church Council, who should have the final say in ringing matters. Too often the incumbent is more concerned with running a successful Youth Club (a feat much more difficult than many clerics realise) and, paradoxically, more attention is paid to extra-clerical activities than to those allied to the church. Bellringing can be a far more rewarding and useful church activity than prowess at table-tennis, or organising a Saturday-night discotheque. In 1971 the magazine *New Christian* published a poem by Basil Saunders demonstrating the pitfalls which may await the too-enthusiastic cleric determined to up-date the conventional church image:

> The ancient crypt is now a coffee-bar
>   With full permission from the PCC

The lych-gate nicely holds the vicar's car,
    The altar's moved halfway from him to me.
He's got a new invention—Series Three,
    His posters tell the story round the town:
'This church is now religion-less and free'
    (I hear the blessed bell-tower's falling down.)

The daily press has broadcast near and far
    The curate's doubts about the Trinity;
Thank God he's not as other curates are—
    He's really just the same as you and me
(Except, of course, he's hooked on LSD)
    He wears a caftan as a BA gown;
Include him in your prayers for those at sea—
    I hear the blessed bell-tower's falling down.

'Honest to God'—we truly think we are
    In touch with all the new theology;
We've ceased to hymn with psalms that evening star,
    No more we run the risk of housemaid's knee;
Discussion groups—ping-pong—a spelling bee
    Each Sunday we conduct with earnest frown;
It's just as well there's no one there to see—
    I hear the blessed bell-tower's falling down.

The number of churches ringing bells on Sundays is slowly
increasing, and most ringers, once reasonably proficient,
remain ringers for life. Even the oldest ringer is continuously
learning, and the art may be acquired at any period of life.
Ringing also tends to continue in families, as the pages of
*Ringing World* demonstrate, but few families can emulate the
record of the Truss family of Marlow, who are recorded as
ringers in 1593 and were still ringing in 1893, 300 years later!
Equally impressive, and also in Buckinghamshire, was the
feat of the six sons of Robert Gibbs of Winslow who rang the
New Year in together as a band forty times in succession during
the eighteenth century.

Canon R. J. Peyton-Burbery, on the other hand, took up
ringing at the age of twenty but did not ring his first quarter
for another seventy years—at Brading, in the Isle of Wight, on

his ninetieth birthday in 1971. A celebration was held after-wards, at which the good canon was presented with a suitably inscribed tankard!

A tankard is a fitting object with which to mark a peal or ringing record, and a church in Surrey recently handed out china mugs to commemorate the re-hanging of its bells. There is nothing the Englishman likes better than belonging to a club or society, and ringers are no exception. Ringers' ties are available, ringers' ash-trays, ringers' car-badges and lapel-buttons, as well as their own journal the *Ringing World* and the *Ringers' Notebook and Diary*.

The inscription on so many tenor bells tells us that 'Death to the Grave Will Summon All', but even at the graveside some ringers are remembered and their deeds recorded on stone for the benefit of posterity. One of the most detailed of all such epitaphs is in the churchyard at Leeds, Kent, and marks the resting-place of the famous ringer, James Barham, who died in 1818 at the age of ninety-three. Part of it reads as follows:

Who from the year 1744 to the year 1804 Rung in Kent and elsewhere 112 peals not less than 5,040 changes in each Peal and called Bobs for most of the Peal And April 7th & 8th 1761 assisted in Ringing 40,320 Bob Major on Leeds Bells in 27 Hours.

James Barham was one of the first to ring 100 peals and he deserves his rest.

Remembered in verse at Nuneaton is David Wheway, who died in 1828:

> Here lieth a ringer
> Beneath this cold clay,
> Who rang many peals
> Bothe serious and gay:
> Through Grandsire and Trebles
> Right well did he range
> Till Death called a 'bob'
> And brought round the last change.

This epitaph can be left to speak for us all.

# APPENDIX

## 1 *Some of Britain's Heaviest Bells*

### (weights are approximate)

#### HUNG FOR CHIMING ONLY

| | |
|---|---|
| St Paul's Cathedral, London  Great Paul | 334cwt |
| Liverpool Cathedral  Great George | 295cwt |
| Westminster  Big Ben | 270cwt |
| York Minster  Great Peter | 216cwt |
| Nottingham Exchange  Little John | 207cwt |
| Bristol University  Great George | 191cwt |
| Manchester Town Hall | 162cwt |
| Buckfast Abbey  Hosannah Bell | 149cwt |
| Beverley Minster, Yorks  Great John | 140cwt |
| Oxford  Great Tom | 127cwt |

#### HUNG FOR RINGING

| | |
|---|---|
| Liverpool Cathedral  Emmanuel | 82cwt |
| Exeter Cathedral  Great Peter | 80cwt |
| Church of the Blessed Sacrament, Heavitree, Exeter | 77cwt |
| Chichester Cathedral | 73cwt |
| Exeter Cathedral  Grandison | 72cwt |
| Canterbury Cathedral  St Dunstan | 70cwt |
| Rugby School Chapel | 64cwt |
| Aberdeen, St Nicholas  No 47 | 63cwt |
| Loughborough War Memorial | 60cwt |

## 2 *Bells Hung for Ringing Outside Britain*

Below is a list of towers where bells are actually rung. A few other towers have bells hung for ringing, but for various reasons (usually of safety) full-circle ringing is not possible.

### AFRICA

Cape Town   Cathedral of St George, 10; St Mary (Woodstock), 8

Durban   St Paul, 8; St Mary (Greyville), 10

Grahamstown, Cape of Good Hope   Cathedral of St Michael, 8

Kilifi, Kenya   Memorial Church of St Thomas, 6

Que-Que, Rhodesia   St Luke, 4

Salisbury, S Rhodesia   St Mary and All Saints Cathedral, 10

### AUSTRALIA AND NEW ZEALAND

Adelaide   St Peter's Cathedral, 8; Town Hall, 8; St Andrew (Walkerville), 6; St Cuthbert (Prospect), 8

Ballarat   City Hall, 8; St Peter, 8

Bendigo   St Paul, 8

Hobart, Tasmania   Holy Trinity, 8; St David's Cathedral, 8

Maitland, NSW   St Paul, 6

Maryborough, Queensland   St Paul, 8

Melbourne   St Patrick's Cathedral, 8; St Paul's Cathedral, 12

Perth   St George's Cathedral, 8

Sydney   All Saints(Parramatta), 6; Christ Church(St Laurence), 6; St Andrew's Cathedral, 10; St Benedict (Broadway), 6; St. James (Turramurra), 6; St Jude (Randwick), 8; St Mary's Basilica, 8; St. Mark (Darling Point), 8; St. Paul (Burwood), 8; St Philip (Church Hill), 8

Yass, NSW   St Clement, 6

Auckland   St Matthew, 6

Christchurch   Christchurch Cathedral, 10; St Paul (Papanui), 5

Hamilton   Cathedral of St Peter (Waikato), 8

## CANADA
Calgary, Alberta   Christ Church, Elbow Park, 8
Mission City, BC   Westminster Abbey, 10
Quebec City   Cathedral of the Holy Trinity, 8; St Matthew, 8
Vancouver, BC   Cathedral of the Holy Rosary, 8
Victoria, BC   Christ Church Cathedral, 8

## ITALY
Rivoli Veronese, N Italy   parish church, 5

## PAKISTAN
Lahore   Cathedral of the Resurrection, 6

## UNITED STATES OF AMERICA
Chicago   The Mitchell Tower of the university, 10
Groton, Mass   school chapel, 10
Hingham, Mass   memorial hall, 10
Houston, Texas   St Thomas, 8
Kent, Connecticut   school chapel, 10
Newcastle, Delaware   parish church, 6
Northampton, Mass   Smith College, 8
Washington, DC   Cathedral of St Peter and St Paul, 10

## 3 Some Technical Terms Used in Ringing

BACKSTROKE  The opposite swing of the bell to 'handstroke' (qv), in which the rope is wound round the perimeter of the wheel, thus leaving only a short length in the ringing-chamber blow, with the sally at about face-level.

BOB  A call by the conductor during change-ringing which causes an odd number of bells to alter their work.

CALL-CHANGES  Changes in the order of ringing which take place only when 'called' by the conductor.

CAMPANOLOGY  The art of bellringing.

CATERS  Changes rung on nine bells. The name is derived from the Latin *quattuor* (four) as four pairs of bells are involved.

CHANGE-RINGING  A system of ringing that causes the bells to change their order of ringing at each pull of the rope.

CHIMING  Causing a bell to sound when in the 'down' position by swinging it through a short arc until the clapper strikes the side. Also used to describe the sounding of a bell by a hammer, either manually or mechanically.

CINQUES  The changes produced on eleven bells, in which *five* pairs interchange at each pull.

CLOCKING  A harmful system of causing a bell to sound by attaching a rope to the clapper and causing it to swing against the side. A frequent cause of a bell cracking.

COMPOSITION  The art of arranging a sequence of sections of patterns of ringing so that no single change is repeated. Certain definite rules are laid down for composing and a transgression of any of these rules results in a 'false' composition.

CONDUCTOR  The person in charge of the ringing for a specific peal or quarter-peal. He must be able to check the work and position of each bell at any given moment, foresee possible errors and extricate ringers from catastrophe without any cessation in the ringing, and call 'bobs' and 'singles' (qv) at the appropriate times.

COURSE  The work performed by a particular bell during the ringing of a method.

COVER  The word used to describe the function of the tenor bell ringing last at each change, when an odd number of bells is being rung to a method.

DODGE  A manoeuvre in change-ringing performed by two bells, one 'hunting up' the other 'hunting down', which change places three times at successive strokes before resuming their normal work.

DOUBLES  Methods rung on five bells in which *two* pairs change at each pull.

EXERCISE  The confraternity of ringers.

EXTENT  The maximum number of changes that can be rung on a given number of bells without repeating one.

FALSE  A term used in composition (qv) when the series of changes transgresses one of the rules, eg when a change is repeated. Also used to describe a bell that rings too soon at handstroke or backstroke.

FIRING  Pulling the ropes so that all the bells strike and sound at the same time. Sometimes used at weddings, and in the past as an alarm bell.

FIXED BELL  A bell which does the same work throughout successive courses and is unaffected by the calling of bobs or singles (qv).

GRANDSIRE  One of the earliest known systems of change-ringing. It is normally pronounced 'Grandser'.

HANDSTROKE  The reverse swing of the bell which allows the maximum length of rope to descend to the ringing chamber after the backstroke (qv).

HOME  The position of the bell when it occupies the same place as it does in rounds (qv). All the bells are said to be 'home' when rounds are struck as the final change in a method.

HUNT  The passage of any bell away from the 'lead' position or towards it, ie either 'hunting up' or 'hunting down'. Also the name given to the bell, usually the treble, that performs this work without variation in the course of a method.

LEAD  The bell that strikes first in any change is said to lead.

MAJOR  A method in which eight bells are involved in changing.

MAXIMUS  A method in which twelve bells are involved in changing.

METHOD  A series of changes rung in an order that has been standardised and named.

MINIMUS  A method in which four bells are involved in changing.

MINOR  A method in which six bells are involved in changing.

MUFFLED  The sound deadened by the attaching of a leather pad to the striking face of the clapper; often used at funerals. When only one face is so treated the bells are 'half-muffled' and when both faces are treated the bells are 'fully-muffled', though this latter procedure is rare.

OBSERVATION BELL  A bell, usually the heaviest included in the change being rung, whose appearance at a certain point, either alone or in combination with other bells, acts as a sign that the method is proceeding correctly.

PEAL  A series of changes rung according to the rules, of not less than 5,040 changes on seven bells and not less than 5,000 on eight or more bells. The word is used incorrectly by non-ringers (a) in describing any ringing of bells, eg 'a wedding peal was rung', and (b) in describing the bells themselves, eg 'there is a peal of eight bells in the tower'. The correct term is 'there is a *ring* of eight bells in the tower'.

PLACE  The position in the order of ringing of a bell at any particular change, and which can alter at each change. Ringing immediately after the lead bell a bell is said to ring 'in second's place' and so on.

PLAIN BOB  The name given to what is probably the earliest system of change-ringing invented.

PRICKING OUT  Writing down changes in rows of figures corresponding to the bells, one row below the other at each change, so that the work of each bell can be studied in isolation.

QUEENS  A change in which all the odd-numbered bells sound

first in succession followed by the even bells, eg (on eight bells) 13572468. Also known as 'odds-and-evens'.

RING  *See* PEAL.

RINGING UP  The raising of the bells from their normal downward-facing position to the upside-down position in which they remain until ringing starts. Ringing up 'in peal' is performing this manoeuvre so that from the start the bells are sounding in their correct order, though with a longer and longer interval between the strokes as the arc of the swing increases. Ringing down is the reverse procedure after ringing has ceased, and again doing this 'in peal' is maintaining the correct order in the sound of the bells until they are all down.

ROPE-SIGHT  The art of recognising the position and intended path of other bells by judging the position of their respective sallies.

ROUNDS  The ringing of bells in their natural order, from the lightest (the treble) to the heaviest (the tenor).

ROYAL  A method in which ten bells are involved in changing.

SALLY  A fluffy, striped 3ft section of coloured material inserted into the bellrope just before its end. It is used partly to obtain a better grip in ringing, but is also a visual aid in rope-sight (qv).

SETTING A BELL  Pulling the rope just hard enough to let the bell stop in its upside-down position.

SILENT PEAL  A peal rung without a conductor and with nobody 'calling' or giving any vocal assistance.

SINGLE  A 'call' given by a conductor which causes an even number of bells to alter their normal course.

SKELETON COURSE  A way of 'pricking out' (qv) a method in which only the treble bell and one other is marked by number, the work of the other bells being represented by dots.

SURPRISE  The name given to certain kinds of methods in which the work of the bells is highly elaborated.

STAND  The 'call' given by the conductor when he wishes the ringing to cease and indicates that each bell must be 'set' at the next handstroke.

TENOR  The heaviest and deepest bell in a ring, and that with the numerically highest number.

TIED BELL  A bell in which a piece of wood is wedged between the clapper and the bell to stop it sounding. Often used in instructing learners in the early stages of handling a bell.

TITTUMS  A change in which the light and heavy bells strike alternately. On eight bells this would produce a sequence of: 1 5 2 6 3 7 4 8 .

TOUCH  Any ringing in a method shorter than a quarter peal.

TREBLE  The lightest bell in a ring with the highest note. When ringing in rounds commences it is customary for the treble ringer to call 'Treble's going—gone!' when the bell is pulled 'off' to alert the other ringers.

TRIPLES  Changes rung on seven bells with *three* pairs of bells changing.

TRUE  The description of any composition or performance which conforms exactly to the rules laid down.

WHOLE-PULL  The double pull of the rope which produces first the handstroke and then the backstroke. Either of these alone is called a 'half-pull' and in normal ringing a change occurs at each one.

WRONG  A term usually used to describe what has happened when the clapper of a bell (often the tenor) begins swinging out of rhythm with the bell itself and therefore sounds out of step. This may happen as the bell is being rung up, in which case the bell is said to have gone up 'wrong'.

# BIBLIOGRAPHY

Allen, F. J. *Great Church Towers of England* (1932)

Camp, J. *Discovering Bellringing* (Shire Publications, 1968)

Central Council for Church Bell Ringers. *Beginners' Handbook* (1970)

Coleman, S. N. *Bells: Their History, Legends, Making and Uses* (1928)

Cooper, J. E. *Bellringers and Bellringing* (1950)

Dove, R. *Bellringers' Guide to the Church Bells of Britain* (W. Viggers, 1968 latest edition, revised every six or seven years. Includes foreign bells)

Frost, A. (ed). *Towers and Belfries* (Central Council for Church Bell Ringers, 1973)

Harrison, R. *Bells of the Isles* (1943)

HMSO. *The Story of Big Ben* (1959)

Howard, H. M. *Bellfounding* (Gillett and Johnston Ltd, 1948)

Hughes, A. A. *Bellfounding—From the Armada to the Great War* (Whitechapel Bell Foundry, 1920)

Hughes, D. *The Whitechapel Bell Foundry—1570 to 1970* (Whitechapel Bell Foundry, 1970)

Ingram, T. *Bells in England* (1954)

Lewty, A. *Church Bells* (1932)

Morris, E. *Bells of All Nations* (1951)

—— *Towers and Bells in Britain* (1955)

Price, P. *Campanology, Europe 1945–47* (1948)

Stedman, Fabian. *Tintinnalogia* (1668; facsimile, Heffer & Sons Ltd, 1968)

Taylor's of Loughborough. *The Taylor Family* (1933)

—— *The Taylor Bell Foundry* (1971)

Thurlow, A. G. *Church Bells and Ringers of Norwich* (Jarrold & Sons, 1947)

Trollope, J. A. *The College Youths—A History* (1937)

Tufts, Nancy P. *The Art of Handbell Ringing* (USA 1961, London 1962)

Vesey, N. *Church Bells and the Art of Ringing* (1950)

### ARTICLES AND PERIODICALS

*Encylopedia Britannica*—articles under 'Bells' and 'Bell Founding'

*Grove's Dictionary of Music and Musicians*—articles under 'Bells', 'Carillons' and 'Change-ringing'

*Ringing World*, published weekly by the Central Council of Church Bell Ringers

Various publications of the Central Council of Church Bell Ringers

# ACKNOWLEDGEMENTS

Apart from my debt to the authors and publishers of many of the works listed I am particularly grateful to the following individuals for their advice and assistance: Mr C. W. Denyer, editor of *Ringing World*; Mr Douglas Hughes, director of the Whitechapel Bell Foundry; Mr Paul Taylor, director of Taylor's Bell Foundry; and Mr Frederick Sharpe, FSA, for assistance with the photographic material.

My thanks go also to the many ringers from all parts of Britain who have given me valuable information and allowed me the benefit of their wide experience.

# INDEX